PHYSICAL EDUCATION FRAMEWORK

for California
Public Schools
Kindergarten
Through
Grade Twelve

Publishing Information

When the *Physical Education Framework* was adopted by the California State Board of Education on September 11, 1992, the members of the State Board were the following: Joseph H. Stein, President; Gerti B. Thomas, Vice-President; Joseph D. Carrabino, Irene Cheng, Kathryn Dronenburg, Yvonne W. Larsen, Dorothy J. Lee, Frank R. Light, S. William Malkasian, Marion McDowell, and Benjamin F. Montoya. The framework was developed by the Physical Education Curriculum Framework and Criteria Committee and was recommended by the Curriculum Development and Supplemental Materials Commission to the State Board of Education for adoption. (See the Acknowledgments for the names of the committee members and others who contributed significantly to this publication.)

This publication was prepared for printing by staff members of the Bureau of Publications: editing, Edward O'Malley; design and layout, Paul Lee; typesetting, Carey Johnson.

The framework was published by the Department of Education, 721 Capitol Mall, Sacramento, California (mailing address: P.O. Box 944272, Sacramento, CA 94244-2720). It was printed by the Office of State Printing and distributed under the provisions of the Library Distribution Act and *Government Code* Section 11096.

ISBN 0-8011-1065-3

Ordering Information

Copies of this publication are available for $6.75 each, plus sales tax for California residents, from the Bureau of Publications, Sales Unit, California Department of Education, P.O. Box 271, Sacramento, CA 95812-0271; FAX (916) 323-0823. See page 92 for complete information on payment, including credit card purchases.

A list of other publications available from the Department appears at the back of this publication. A complete list may be obtained by writing to the address given above or by calling the Sales Unit at (916) 445-1260.

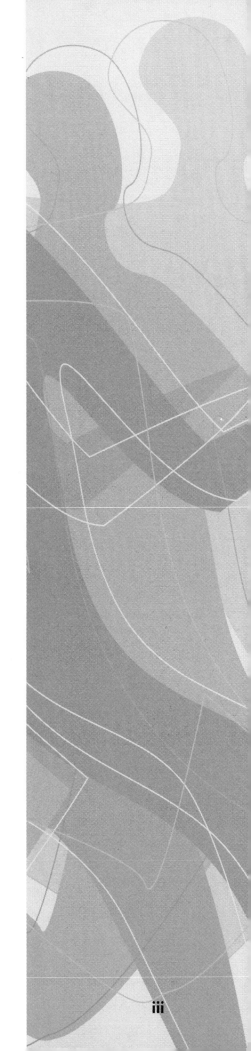

CONTENTS

The 1994 *Physical Education Framework for California Public Schools, Kindergarten Through Grade Twelve,* describes a sequential, developmental, age-appropriate physical education program designed to provide students with the knowledge and ability needed to maintain an active, healthy life-style. It expands on the vision of the 1986 *Handbook for Physical Education* that physical education be an integral part of the school's educational program. The new framework calls for an effective physical education program that balances and contributes to children's academic learning. It also expresses the conviction that educators, working together with students, the family, and the community, can successfully guide our children and youths to discover their talents and develop the knowledge and skills needed to use those talents in achieving personal goals.

Unfortunately, as evidenced by the results of the *California Physical and Health-related Fitness Test* for 1993, the physical fitness of California's students has not improved much over the past four years. Educators and parents must recognize that students of all ages need to be as physically active as they are able to be in order to stay healthy. Students need physical education every day. It is also important that students have the knowledge and understanding needed to participate in physical activities correctly, safely, and to the best of their ability. For example, students should be able to enjoy such activities as running or playing softball not only because they enjoy the activity but also because they understand and are applying the knowledge needed to achieve their highest level of physical performance.

The *Physical Education Framework* was developed by the Physical Education Curriculum Framework and Criteria Committee under the direction of the Curriculum Development and Supplemental Materials Commission. The framework committee determined the basic nature of the framework and presented its draft to the state's Curriculum Development and Supplemental Materials Commission in March, 1992. More than a thousand copies of the draft were then sent for review to educators in school districts, offices of county superintendents of schools, and institutions of higher education throughout California. The draft was also sent out to the public on request, and each response was reviewed, analyzed, and incorporated into the draft when appropriate. In May, 1992, the Curriculum Commission recommended that the draft be sent to the State Board of Education for adoption. After further revisions were made at the request of the State Board, the framework was adopted in September, 1992.

This new *Physical Education Framework,* which provides philosophical direction and perspectives on curriculum and instruction, is an important resource for curriculum planners, decision makers, teachers, and parents to use in developing strong instructional programs. Through collaborative efforts we can prepare our children to be healthy and fit for the rest of their lives.

WILLIAM D. DAWSON
*Acting State Superintendent
of Public Instruction*

JOSEPH H. STEIN
*President
California State Board of Education*

HARVEY HUNT
*Deputy Superintendent
Curriculum and Instructional
Leadership Branch*

FRED TEMPES
*Associate Superintendent and Director
Curriculum, Instruction, and
Assessment Division*

JANE HENDERSON
*Assistant Superintendent and Director
Interagency Children and Youth
Services Division*

ACKNOWLEDGMENTS

The *Physical Education Framework* was developed by the Physical Education Curriculum Framework and Criteria Committee under the direction of the Curriculum Development and Supplemental Materials Commission. Members of the committee are listed as follows:

Margaret Leeds (Chair), Assistant Principal, Beverly Hills High School, Beverly Hills Unified School District

Dan Cariaga, Adapted Physical Education Program Specialist, San Luis Obispo County Office of Education

Bonnie Mohnsen, Coordinator for Physical Education and Health Education, Montebello Unified School District

Nancy Sanchez-Spears, Physical Education Specialist, Urbita Elementary School, San Bernardino City Unified School District

Gail Zettel-McShane, Physical Education Teacher, Pomolita Middle School, Ukiah Unified School District

Members of the Health and Physical Education Subject Matter Committee, Curriculum Development and Supplemental Materials Commission, responsible for overseeing the development and the field review of the framework were the following:

Del Alberti, Superintendent, Washington Unified School District

Gloria Blanchette, Teacher, Sam Brannan Middle School, Sacramento City Unified School District

Note: Titles and locations of all persons listed in the Acknowledgments were current when this document was being prepared.

Daniel Chernow, Pacific Theatres Corporation, Los Angeles

Bruce Fisher, Teacher, Fortuna Elementary School, Fortuna Union Elementary School District

Eugene Flores (Chair, 1992), Teacher, Arroyo Grande High School, Lucia Mar Unified School District

Harriett Harris, Teacher, Del Mar Elementary School, Fresno Unified School District

Charles Kloes, Teacher, Beverly Hills High School, Beverly Hills Unified School District

Charles Koepke (deceased), Teacher, Upland Junior High School, Upland Unified School District

Tom Vasta (Chair, 1991), Science Resource Teacher, Elk Grove Unified School District

VivianLee Ward, Teacher, Sequoia High School, Sequoia Union High School District

Overall coordination of the development, field review, and preparation of the *Physical Education Framework* was guided by **Glen Thomas,** Director, Curriculum Frameworks and Instructional Resources Office, California Department of Education.

Staff support from the California Department of Education was provided by the following:

M. Jeanne Bartelt, Consultant, Health Promotion Office

Janet Chladek, Consultant, Curriculum Frameworks and Instructional Resources Office

Ples Griffin, Administrator, Health Promotion Office

Pat Valladao, Consultant, Health Promotion Office

Appreciation is extended to **Hank Resnik** for assistance in writing and editing.

This *Physical Education Framework,* which charts a course in physical education for children in kindergarten through grade twelve, will remain relevant for many years to come. As we approach a new century, it is time for us to revisit the vision and context needed for success in physical education, which has never been more important and necessary than it is today.

Physical Education and Children's Well-Being

The first and perhaps most important aspect of physical education is the direct bearing it has on children's physical, mental, and social well-being. The child who is well educated physically is likely to become a healthy adult who is motivated to remain healthy.

Although adults are often well informed about health and pursue healthy life-styles that include good nutrition, exercise, physical activity, and fitness, their children's physical health and well-being are frequently a cause for concern. Recognizing the threat of a sedentary life-style inherent in postindustrial work patterns, large numbers of adults can be found jogging, walking, eating healthy foods, and seeking out ways to incorporate movement and activity into their daily routines. But at the same time alarming numbers of children and youths, often lacking appropriate adult supervision, can be found in front of television sets on sunny weekday afternoons munching on snack foods.

This problem is compounded by approaches to physical education that have traditionally emphasized competition, games, sports, and native athletic ability, favoring those who are most talented and leaving the less able to view themselves as outsiders who will never make the grade. Our

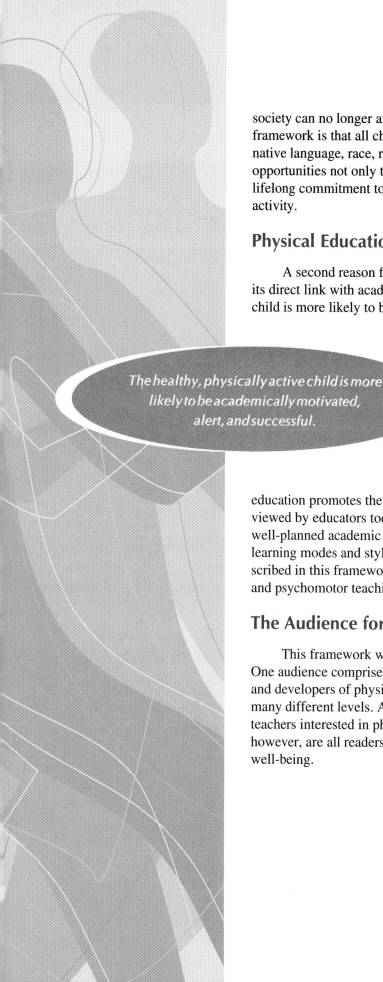

society can no longer afford that approach. A principal theme of this framework is that all children—regardless of disability, ethnicity, gender, native language, race, religion, or sexual orientation—must be given opportunities not only to succeed in physical education but to develop a lifelong commitment to the pleasure and the health benefits of physical activity.

Physical Education and Academic Success

A second reason for the importance of physical education today is its direct link with academic learning. The healthy, physically active child is more likely to be academically motivated, alert, and successful.

The healthy, physically active child is more likely to be academically motivated, alert, and successful.

In the preschool and primary years, there are direct links between active play, physical agility and coordination, and academic success. As children grow older and enter adolescence, healthy physical activity becomes integral to their self-concept and their ability to take on new intellectual, social, and emotional challenges. Throughout, physical education promotes the social skills and cooperation that are increasingly viewed by educators today as essential for success in school. Just as any well-planned academic curriculum takes into account a wide range of learning modes and styles, the physical education curriculum, as described in this framework, emphasizes a variety of cognitive, affective, and psychomotor teaching and learning strategies.

The Audience for This Framework

This framework was developed for several overlapping audiences. One audience comprises physical education teachers and the planners and developers of physical education programs and resources—all at many different levels. Another is those elementary and secondary teachers interested in physical education. Perhaps most important, however, are all readers who are concerned about children's health and well-being.

CHAPTER ONE

A VISION
for
PHYSICAL
EDUCATION

CHAPTER ONE

This *Physical Education Framework* is based on the premise that the quality and productivity of each individual's life can be enhanced through participation in a comprehensive, sequential physical education system that promotes physical, mental, emotional, and social well-being. Education implies a focus on the whole person as opposed to a narrow range of skills or abilities. It means teaching children how to apply new knowledge and how to become lifelong learners. The concept of lifelong learning is as relevant to physical education as it is to other areas of instruction.

A physically educated person is one who has mastered the necessary movement skills to participate confidently in many different forms of physical activity, values physical fitness, and understands that both are intimately related to health and well-being.[1] The most basic element of a child's development is learning to move. Even before birth children begin learning to move and learning through movement. The process continues throughout childhood and early adolescence. Movement skills are central to physical education at all grade levels.

Physical education addresses the child's fundamental need for regular physical activity to remain healthy and promotes many of the attitudes and behaviors that reduce health risks, including development of

---

[1] The definition of a *physically educated person* used throughout this framework corresponds closely to that of the American Alliance for Health, Physical Education, Recreation, and Dance (AAHPERD) and the National Association for Sport and Physical Education (NASPE). It defines the physically educated person as one who *has* the necessary movement skills, *is* physically fit, *does* participate regularly in physical activity, *knows* the implications and benefits of involvement in physical activity, and *values* physical activity and its contribution to a healthy lifestyle. See Appendix A for the complete AAHPERD/NASPE definition.

an understanding of the need for appropriate nutrition and exercise. A quality physical education program can motivate students to maintain healthy eating habits and regular physical activity. A well-planned physical education program guides students to becoming motivated to attain optimum health through regular use of new knowledge and skills.

Helping All Children and Youths Become Physically Educated

This framework provides the planners and developers of physical education programs and resources with a clearly articulated set of concepts and strategies that form the foundation of a comprehensive physical education system for kindergarten through grade twelve. It grows out of a vision of physical education being *more* than games, sports, and fitness. The overall aim of such a system is to help *all* children and youths develop into physically educated individuals. This approach is consistent with major directions in the health field generally as articulated in *Healthy People 2000*, a report that identifies 298 specific objectives in 22 priority areas, including physical activity and fitness.[2]

A physically educated person is one who has mastered the necessary movement skills to participate confidently in many different forms of physical activity, values physical fitness, and understands that both are intimately related to health and well-being.

In a society that tends to be mechanized, stress-ridden, and sedentary, the physically educated person is prepared to participate throughout life in appropriate physical activities. He or she can also make choices that will minimize the risks of cardiovascular diseases that afflict one in four people in the United States. For the physically educated person, health and physical well-being are important personal values.

All children and youths need a well-planned physical education program that begins at the earliest grade levels, receives strong support schoolwide, is understood and reinforced at home, and is supported by a comprehensive health education program. All have the potential to achieve an active, healthy life-style.

Developing a Commitment to Physical Activity and Physical Fitness

A slang expression, *couch potato,* aptly describes someone who is the opposite of a physically educated person: unfit, inactive, and oblivious to the basic principles of staying fit and healthy. Ironically, some adults who today lack fitness and health were yesterday's child and

---

[2] *Healthy People 2000: National Health Promotion and Disease Prevention Objectives.* Washington, D.C.: U.S. Department of Health and Human Services, Public Health Service, 1991.

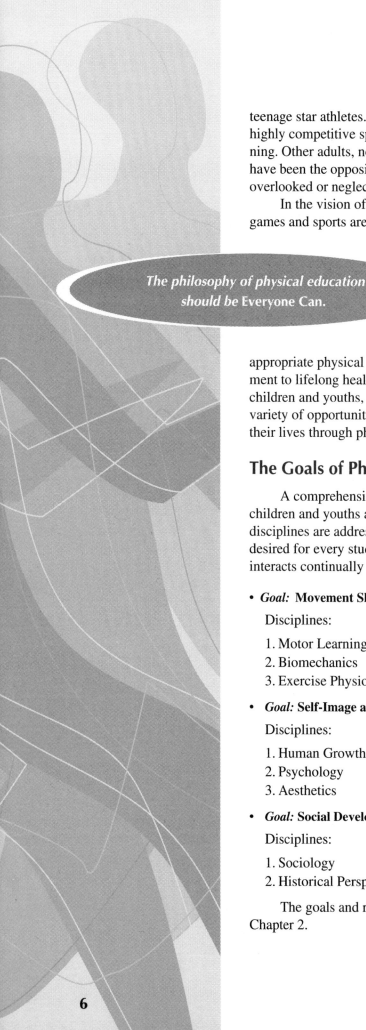

teenage star athletes. In their youth they may have been successful in a highly competitive sport—almost always with one primary goal, winning. Other adults, now leading inactive, unhealthy life-styles, may once have been the opposite. Lacking athletic talent, they may have been overlooked or neglected in physical education classes.

In the vision of physical education presented in this framework, games and sports are a means to an end, not an end in themselves. The philosophy of physical education should be *Everyone Can.* Every child and youth can develop appropriate skills, feel good about his or her body, and relate to others in positive ways.

Many different elements of age-appropriate physical activity and instruction help to develop a commitment to lifelong health, physical activity, and physical education. All children and youths, regardless of their athletic talents, should have a variety of opportunities to participate in physical education and enrich their lives through physical activity.

The philosophy of physical education should be Everyone Can.

The Goals of Physical Education

A comprehensive, articulated physical education system helps children and youths achieve three goals. Within each goal appropriate disciplines are addressed to support the knowledge, skills, and attitudes desired for every student. The three goals are equally important; each interacts continually with the others in a well-planned program.

- *Goal:* **Movement Skills and Movement Knowledge**

  Disciplines:

  1. Motor Learning
  2. Biomechanics
  3. Exercise Physiology and Health-related Physical Fitness

- *Goal:* **Self-Image and Personal Development**

  Disciplines:

  1. Human Growth and Development
  2. Psychology
  3. Aesthetics

- *Goal:* **Social Development**

  Disciplines:

  1. Sociology
  2. Historical Perspectives

The goals and related disciplines are described in more detail in Chapter 2.

Skill and Content Areas

The following skill and content areas support the goals of physical education and are introduced at appropriate ages and grade levels. In addition to developing skills in these various areas, students should be encouraged to acquire understanding and knowledge about the content and skills. They should be able to grasp the *why* as well as the *how* and to understand that the content areas are a vehicle for developing and refining the skills.

Skill Areas

- Sensorimotor and perceptual motor. *Examples:* kinesthetic, visual, tactile, auditory
- Locomotor. *Examples:* walking, running, jumping, hopping, galloping, skipping
- Nonlocomotor. *Examples:* swinging/swaying, bending/stretching, pushing/pulling, twisting/turning
- Balance. *Examples:* static: stunts, balance equipment; dynamic: tricycle, unicycle, scooter, beams
- Eye-hand coordination. *Examples:* gross motor: throwing, catching, bouncing; fine motor: pouring, clapping, cutting, grasping
- Eye-foot coordination. *Examples:* kicking, trapping, dribbling, punting, rhythmic movement
- General coordination. *Examples:* swinging, climbing, sliding, jumping rope, tumbling
- Creative movement. *Examples:* rhythmic walking, swaying, moving to music, mirroring movement

Content Areas

- Rhythms and Dance
- Aquatics
- Combatives (e.g., self-defense and fencing)
- Outdoor Education
- Gymnastics and Tumbling
- Individual and Dual Sports
- Team Sports
- Mechanics of Body Movement
- Effects of Physical Activity on Dynamic Health

These skill and content areas are the basis of physical education. For example, developing a sense of rhythm helps children do better in a variety of activities and enhances a sense of flow and coordination. At all levels of the physical education curriculum, the skill areas are taught and reinforced through the content.

Cognitive learning is an inherent part of the skill and content areas. For example, students learn the application of Newton's laws in developing rotational skills, balance, and spin. This knowledge helps to reinforce and strengthen their understanding of the skills and their ability to use them. Throughout the physical education curriculum, children should be

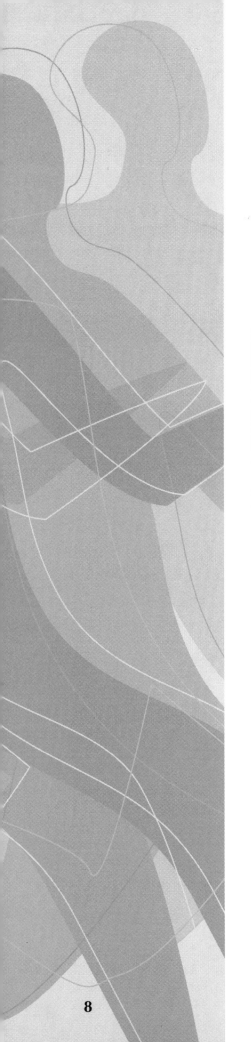

encouraged to observe their own and others' behavior and to process information. Although children do learn through trial and error, they also benefit from guided discovery and development of an understanding of skills and content.

The skill and content areas, together with their relationship to the goals and disciplines, are presented in more detail in Chapter 3.

Counteracting Myths About Physical Education

The vision of physical education and the physically educated individual presented in this framework counteracts common myths about physical education:

Myth

Physical education is intended to help students achieve excellence in games and sports.

Framework vision

Physical education is a multifaceted process that teaches a wide range of skills and activities with the aim of the students' becoming physically educated, physically fit, able to enjoy a variety of physical activities, and committed to lifelong health and physical well-being. It is a continuing process of articulated, sequential development of skills, talents, attitudes, and behaviors.

Myth

Physical education is not an integral part of the school's curriculum. It is a frill.

Framework vision

Physical education is closely connected to and supports the other disciplines. Physical education is an integral component of the school curriculum. It involve students directly in thinking, creating meaning, and learning how to learn.

Myth

Physical education focuses on the more athletically gifted.

Framework vision

All children have the potential to become physically educated, and an effective physical education program will reach all children regardless of their talents, skills, or limitations.

Myth

Physical education should be similar to training—highly skill- and drill-oriented. It should be mainly a mechanical process.

Framework vision

In physical education emphasis must be placed on a broad spectrum of learning and personal development. Learning involves thinking and feeling, being active and processing information, not just using skills. Education encompasses much more than training.

Myth

Children should carry out a variety of physical fitness activities but do not need to understand why they are doing so.

Framework vision

Learning cognitively is as important to physical education as learning specific movement skills. Students need to know why they are learning skills in physical education and how they are benefiting personally. Then they will be more likely to accept responsibility for improving skills on their own and enjoying the benefits of physical education over the long term.

Myth

Physical education programs may be detrimental to doing one's best in a particular activity. It is important to focus on a specific activity (or sport) in order to do really well.

Framework vision

A well-planned, comprehensive physical education system helps children and youths develop all their abilities and talents rather than focus exclusively on a narrow range. Because children change and grow over time, they should be encouraged to become well rounded. They should be encouraged to become proficient in and appreciate a wide variety of physical activities from which they can choose wisely.

Myth

Because there are always winners and losers in games and sports, physical education must emphasize competition to prepare children for participation in the real world.

Framework vision

Although teachers are aware of the nature of competition, they do not require higher levels of competition from children before they are ready. Further, competition can take different forms. Activities in physical education programs may emphasize self-improvement, participation, and cooperation instead of winning or losing.

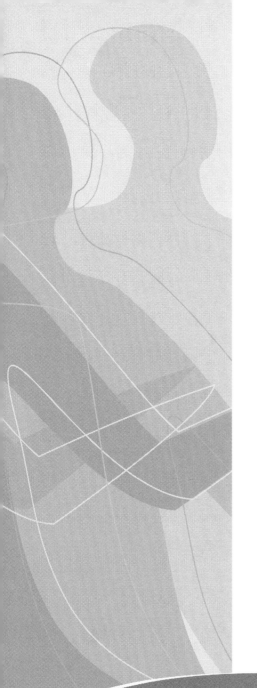

Major Premises of This Framework

This framework is based on a set of major premises that permeate every chapter and should be clearly understood by anyone planning or developing a physical education program for children in kindergarten through grade twelve:

- A well-planned physical education program is sequential, developmental, and age-appropriate.
- An effective physical education program should be governed by the vision for physical education described in this framework. It does not consist of just games and sports.
- An effective physical education program balances and contributes to children's academic learning. It is not separate and distinct from the core curriculum. Neither is participation in a specialized athletic sport an adequate substitute for a comprehensive physical education system.
- Physical education programs should help children and youths develop a lifelong commitment to their own physical well-being, health, and fitness, with a clear emphasis on a variety of pleasurable physical activities and an active life-style.
- The three goals presented in this framework are central to an effective physical education program. No single goal should be emphasized to the exclusion of the other goals.
- Schools need to have a well-planned and well-supported physical education program for children in kindergarten through grade twelve. To do so requires a commitment of leadership, staff, and resources.

Physical Education and Competition

Excessive emphasis on the competitive aspect of sports, games, and athletic achievement conflicts with the goals of physical education. However, normal competition is an inherent part of American life and can be an element in a child's intrinsic motivation to do his or her best in any physical activity. It can also be an arena in which the *I, we,* and *team* concepts join together and take on added meaning.

A common mistake is to emphasize competition too much while children are still quite young.

A common mistake is to emphasize competition too much while children are still quite young. Children are able to create their own competition in normal play. In early childhood children should be encouraged to recognize the intrinsic reward of doing one's personal best. Only at about the age of ten or eleven are they ready physiologically, socially, and emotionally to participate in other levels of competitive activities.

A program oriented to the success of every child provides a nonthreatening environment in which a child is never subjected to the humiliation of being chosen last or being dropped from a team. Attention should be focused on the uniqueness and abilities of each person.

Neither winning nor losing is the crux of physical education. What matters is that competition equates with making the most of one's physical potential and capabilities in a positive, meaningful way. The goal of the physical educator should be not to identify winners but to make winners of ordinary students.

Physical Education and Health Education

A well-planned physical education program is one component of a comprehensive school health system. That system, which comprises an organized set of policies, procedures, and activities designed to protect and promote the health and well-being of students and staff, includes the following components:

- Health Education
- Physical Education
- Health Services
- Nutrition Services
- Psychological and Counseling Services
- Safe and Healthy School Environment
- Health Promotion for Staff
- Parent and Community Involvement

As two components in a comprehensive school health system, physical education and health education should complement each other. However, the ways in which they are separate and distinct must be recognized. Health education, as described in the *Health Framework for California Public Schools* (1994), focuses on four unifying ideas of health literacy. Health literacy is "the capacity of an individual to obtain, interpret, and understand basic health information and services and the competence to use such information and services in ways which are health-enhancing."[3] The four unifying ideas are the following:

- Acceptance of personal responsibility for lifelong health
- Respect for and promotion of the health of others
- An understanding of the process of growth and development
- Informed use of health-related information, products, and services

Physical education focuses on three goals: (1) movement skills and movement knowledge; (2) self-image and personal development; and (3) social development. Where physical education differs most distinctly from health education is in the emphasis that physical education places on teaching students how to move. (See "Movement Skills and Movement Knowledge" in Chapter 2.)

What matters is that competition equates with making the most of one's physical potential and capabilities in a positive, meaningful way.

[3] "Report of the 1990 Joint Committee on Health Education Terminology," *Journal of Health Education,* Vol. 22, No. 2 (1991), 104.

A Governing Metaphor:
The Growth of a Healthy Tree

The development of a physically educated person can be compared with the growth of a tree. Figure 1 illustrates this concept in detail. The roots of the tree correspond to the preschool and primary levels. At this point children are learning the fundamentals of physical education, becoming more skillful, and deriving pleasure from learning new skills through experience with the various content areas. Three fundamentals of physical education that correspond to learning letters in reading and learning numbers in mathematics are central to these levels:

- Locomotion—moving the body from one place to another
- Nonlocomotion—remaining in place and maintaining balance while moving parts of the body
- Object manipulation—including manipulating objects with parts of the body

At the preschool and primary levels, development of physical and motor fitness attributes is emphasized, including agility, flexibility, and coordination. This level emphasizes such basic skills as walking, running, hopping, jumping, sliding, galloping, skipping, catching, throwing, kicking, balancing, bending, and stretching. Also important are such fitness attributes as cardiorespiratory fitness and muscular strength and endurance.

The trunk of the tree corresponds to the upper elementary years. At this level children begin to combine the fundamental skills they have learned in the preschool and primary years and apply and refine the skills in new experiences. At the upper levels of the tree, including the middle school years, children are becoming independent, self-directed learners. They are beginning to internalize the principles of physical education from the earlier grades into a personal commitment to a healthy life-style and physical activity. They participate regularly in a variety of physical activities, take pleasure in both group and individual activities, and have begun to formulate a goal of lifelong health. Throughout, the process engages all aspects of learning: cognitive ("I know"); affective ("I feel"); and psychomotor ("I experience and do").

As the tree branches out at the upper levels, high school students are able to choose and participate freely in team sports, individual sports, aquatics, dance, combatives, fitness, tumbling and gymnastics, and other specific aspects of the physical education curriculum. This is an appropriate time for specializing in particular activities, a time when skills learned at the earlier levels become more meaningful and pleasurable in ways that are both satisfying and complex.

Throughout, the activities are related to children's social development, moving from an emphasis on *I* at the lower levels to *we* at the middle levels and, finally, to a fully developed sense of cooperation and teamwork. It is also appropriate at the upper levels to engage in a variety of activities building social skills.

Fig. 1. Development of a physically educated person

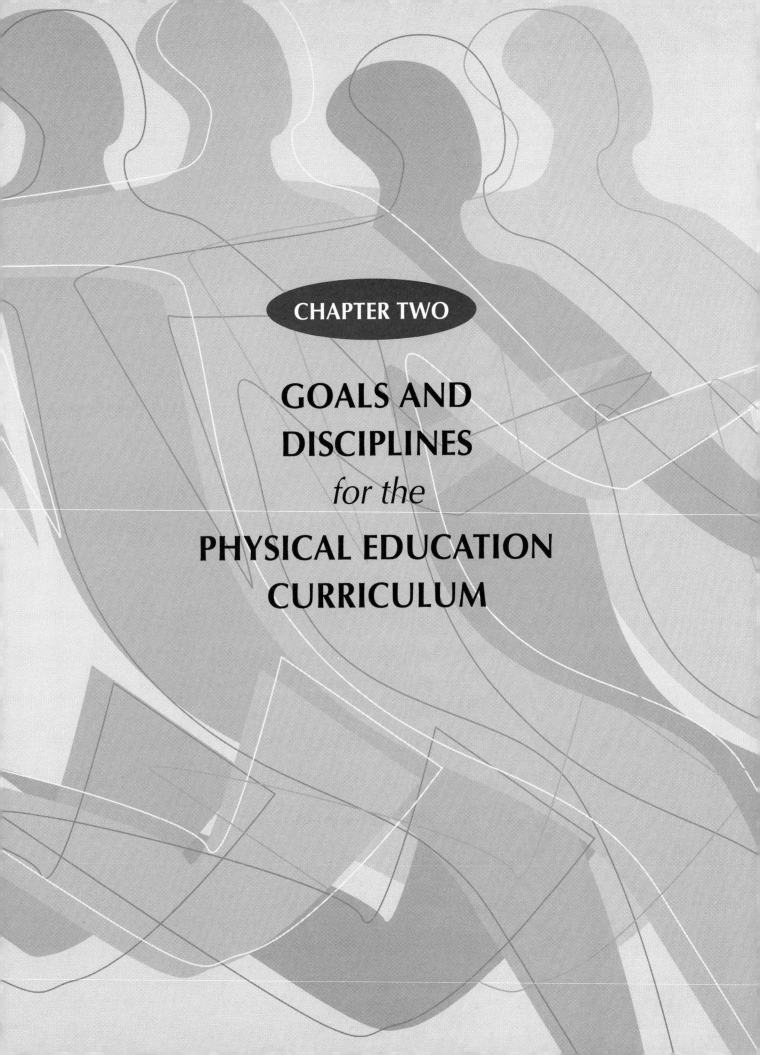

CHAPTER TWO

GOALS AND
DISCIPLINES
for the

PHYSICAL EDUCATION
CURRICULUM

This framework emphasizes three major goals for the physical education curriculum. Supporting and reinforcing each of these goals are underlying disciplines.

Goal: **Movement Skills and Movement Knowledge**

Disciplines:

1. Motor Learning
2. Biomechanics
3. Exercise Physiology and Health-related Physical Fitness

Goal: **Self-Image and Personal Development**

Disciplines:

1. Human Growth and Development
2. Psychology
3. Aesthetics

Goal: **Social Development**

Disciplines:

1. Sociology
2. Historical Perspectives

Throughout the kindergarten through grade twelve curriculum, all three goals of physical education are addressed, together with their respective disciplines. There is a flow of learning from one goal to another and from one grade level to another. Because movement and activity are central to physical education, the goal of movement skills and movement knowledge is the key to a well-planned program. True comprehensiveness can be achieved, however, only through a focus on all three goals.

Within each goal the appropriate disciplines support the knowledge, skills, and attitudes desired for every student. The disciplines are an important part of the knowledge base of physical education, guiding what is taught and when. They provide instructors with both a rationale for the instructional program and specific content.

Movement Skills and Movement Knowledge

Students need to develop effective motor skills and to understand the fundamentals of movement by practicing and analyzing purposeful movement.

The most basic element of the student's learning experience in physical education is learning how to move. The physical education curriculum begins, therefore, by addressing the primary goal of achieving movement skills and movement knowledge. A comprehensive physical education program guides each student in the development of motor skills that allow the student to:

1. Move in a variety of ways.
2. Learn effective and efficient movement appropriate to the student's changing needs.
3. Understand the fundamentals of movement.
4. Appreciate the aesthetics of creative movement.
5. Enjoy movement for movement's sake.
6. Develop all the skills needed to select appropriate activities to develop and maintain a high level of health-related physical fitness.

Movement is the primary medium through which the physical educator reaches and teaches the whole child. Emphasis should be placed on guiding children to discover what they can *do*. They need to develop proficiency in movement skills so that physical activity will be a successful and enjoyable experience that enhances self-image. Moreover, they should have opportunities to participate in expressive and creative movement leading to greater self-realization and personal satisfaction. Experiences in physical education can play a powerful role in influencing a

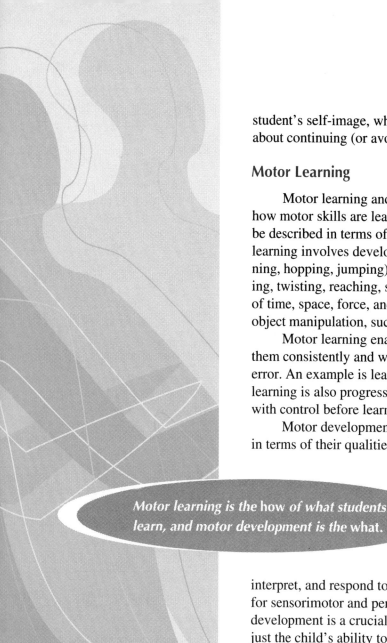

student's self-image, which, in turn, influences *how* that student will feel about continuing (or avoiding) participation in physical activity.

Motor Learning

Motor learning and motor development together are the basis for how motor skills are learned and what they look like. These concepts can be described in terms of the learner and the learning environment. Motor learning involves development of locomotor skills (e.g., walking, running, hopping, jumping) and nonlocomotor skills (e.g., balancing, bending, twisting, reaching, stretching) and an understanding of the qualities of time, space, force, and flow applicable to those skills. It also involves object manipulation, such as catching, throwing, kicking, and juggling.

Motor learning enables students to master skills in order to perform them consistently and well. It involves feedback, judgment, and trial and error. An example is learning how to take aim and hit a mark. Motor learning is also progressive—for example, learning how to bounce a ball with control before learning to dribble.

Motor development refers to what the skills and activities look like in terms of their qualities. Skills and activities can be performed in isolation or as part of a more complex dance, game, sport, or other performance. Motor learning is the *how* of what students learn, and motor development is the *what*. In the elementary grades it is particularly important that children receive, interpret, and respond to visual, auditory, tactile, and kinesthetic stimuli for sensorimotor and perceptual motor feedback. Perceptual motor development is a crucial need in the early grades, influencing more than just the child's ability to move. It also has an important influence on readiness for learning.

> *Motor learning is the* how *of what students learn, and motor development is the* what.

Biomechanics

Biomechanics is the science that examines the internal and external forces acting on a human body and the effects they produce. It involves the study of how the body moves and how such movement is influenced by gravity, friction, and the laws of motion. Knowing how and why movement occurs and whether it is efficient assists in problem solving and enhances understanding of movement and motor skills. This understanding enables students to modify their performance for skill improvement and determine the most appropriate technique for each motor skill.

Key terms include *Newton's laws of motion, center of gravity, force projection and absorption, buoyancy, spin, rotational mechanics, levers, vectors,* and *motion.* Through experimentation or guided discovery, students learn that by applying biomechanical principles to physical activity, they can improve their skills and performance.

Exercise Physiology and Health-related Physical Fitness

Exercise physiology expands the student's knowledge of the physical self through the study of the human body. Learning progresses from the preschooler's awareness of body parts to the more advanced study of body systems, the ways in which the systems interact, and the effects of exercise on those systems. Students gain an understanding of the importance of developing and maintaining optimum fitness in the areas of cardiorespiratory endurance, flexibility, muscular strength and endurance, and body composition. They learn not only *what* to do but *why* to do it and *how* to do it appropriately and effectively.

An important component of exercise physiology is knowing what kind of exercise is needed, how much is needed, and how it is to be performed. Instruction in the principles of physical fitness training should address the issues of frequency, intensity, and time (FIT) as well as specific types of exercise and their effects on the body. It should prepare the student for designing an appropriate personal exercise plan.

At each grade level students are expected to meet the criteria for health-related fitness established in the *California Physical and Health-related Fitness Test* or other comparable tests. These criteria often identify the threshold level of fitness to be attained in each fitness component for students five to eighteen years of age so that the risk of disease or disability associated with sedentary, unhealthy life-styles will be lessened. Throughout, the emphasis should be not so much on meeting the minimal criteria but on doing one's personal best and setting appropriate goals for improvement.

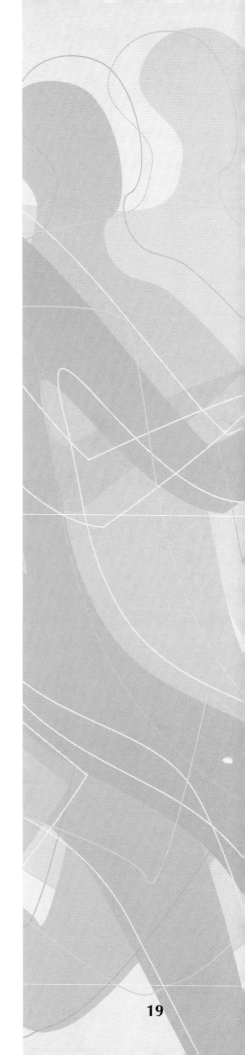

Self-Image and Personal Development

Students develop and maintain a positive self-image and strive to become the best that they can be through planned physical activities.

From childhood through adulthood individuals are always developing their self-image and becoming the best that they can be. A child's self-perception begins in infancy through interaction with others. The ability to move effectively is closely associated with a child's self-perception. Because self-image has a direct bearing on one's ability and willingness to learn in any situation, the physical education curriculum must be carefully planned and implemented to help students learn to

move effectively and efficiently, thereby enhancing a positive self-image and helping students to achieve their best.

Students who lack appropriate movement skills may not feel good about themselves or about physical activity and will often choose not to be physically active. To realize their full potential through physical education, students should be encouraged to appraise their skills and talents realistically, make a personal commitment to a plan for improving those skills, take appropriate risks to achieve their goals, and persevere.

This framework recommends a move away from inappropriate competitive activities, however, including emphasis on winners and losers. Instead, the framework emphasizes the motto *Every Student a Winner.* Students should be helped to discover what they can do and appreciate their own uniqueness and that of others.

Human Growth and Development

Children experience the stages of growth and development at different rates. When they learn that individuals are not automatically considered wrong or bad if they develop more slowly or more rapidly than their peers, they are better prepared to accept individual differences. At the same time certain aspects of physical development are relatively common at specific age and grade levels. An understanding of the body-type variations of endomorph (fat), mesomorph (muscular), and ectomorph (thin) can help students accept capabilities and limitations that may be a function of body type. Therefore, an understanding of developmentally appropriate activities is necessary.

Psychology

Positive emotional development is closely related to good feelings resulting from movement in physical education activities. One aspect of positive emotional development is learning to acknowledge, accept, and appreciate differences between oneself and others with regard to abilities and achievement. Self-acceptance, which is enhanced as students take pride in personal excellence and try to improve their performance, is closely connected with developing a sense of personal responsibility. By overcoming physical challenges and other obstacles at each level of development, students acquire the confidence they need to progress further and to take on new challenges.

Aesthetics

Physical education reinforces self-confidence and self-image by providing students with a sense of accomplishment and aesthetic pleasure in mastering and applying movement skills. This effect is not limited to superior levels but can happen at all levels of competence.

Participating in physical activity helps students develop a heightened awareness of how the body feels in movement, how it can be trained to move more efficiently, and why it needs regular vigorous exercise to achieve and maintain good health. In turn, a healthy body moves more gracefully and effectively for longer periods of time. The healthy person feels good about moving and enjoys a sense of exhilaration in movement.

Across the ages every culture has expressed itself through dance and movement. The philosophy, art, life-style, political life, and religion of diverse cultures have all been translated into movement in rituals, games, or dances. All are potential means of achieving creative self-expression.

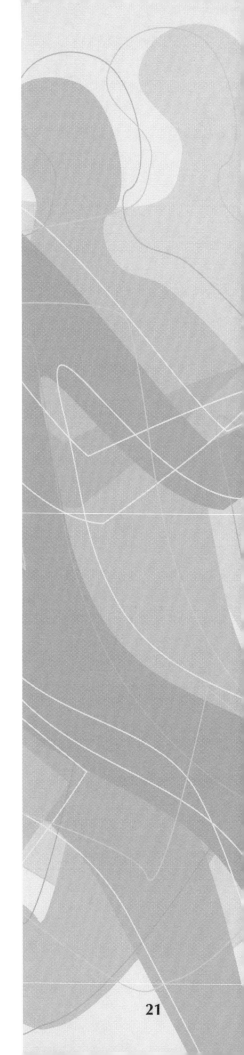

Social Development

Students develop appropriate social behaviors by working independently and with others during planned physical activity.

Participating in physical activity as a member of a group is central to children's acceptance of responsibility for their health and physical well-being and a lifelong appreciation of physical activity. Through guided experiences all students should develop the skills needed to participate with others in a productive manner not only in physical education activities but in all other aspects of social interaction as well.

Working with another student or in small groups, students can support each other in meeting challenges, testing each other's skills, and living, working, and playing together harmoniously. They learn that effective group work depends on cooperation and fair competition. They also learn to assess situations and to identify and solve problems.

When competition is kept in perspective so that the students can achieve their full potential, they learn to value fair play and control their emotions. By emphasizing fair competition and good sportsmanship, physical education contributes to the students' development of a personal code of ethics that leads to making morally responsible decisions.

The acquisition of positive social skills also contributes to the mental health and well-being of each student by combating risk factors for substance abuse and other social problems. All students can learn positive social skills, which must be modeled daily by instructional leaders.

Sociology

Sociology, a dynamic process by which the culture and norms of a society are transmitted, includes learning the society's norms, roles, values, and expectations as well as studying human relationships and social behavior.

In physical education sociology relates to developing and applying positive social norms and values not only to physical education activities but also to intramural athletics and other school activities. The learning and acceptance of social norms help students to develop an acceptance not just of rules but of the need for fairness and equity.

Sociology also emphasizes learning to respect others, appreciate the diversity of our society, and recognize the importance of understanding other cultures. Closely associated with these aspects of social interaction is the need to understand the development of appropriate social behavior and etiquette in a variety of settings on and off the playing field.

Historical Perspectives

Physical education has the longest history of all educational efforts. Understanding history contributes to both the student's and the instructor's awareness of the rationale underlying physical education today. Physical education has changed considerably over the years. During the early Middle Ages, for example, physical development was considered secondary to development of the mind. With the Renaissance, however, came a new emphasis on the development of the whole person. In the eighteenth century the importance of developing both a sound body and a sound mind was emphasized, reflecting a return to the philosophy of ancient Greece.

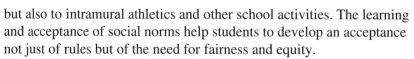

Our contemporary awareness of the importance of all aspects of health has led to a comprehensive view of physical education emphasizing development of a healthy body, mind, and spirit.

Even in our own century, numerous trends have affected physical education. Different games, sports, and activities have been in favor at different times. Nevertheless, the essentials of movement and coordination underlying these games are often the same (e.g., combatives). Over a period of decades, emphasis has shifted from wrestling and boxing to the martial arts.

Our contemporary awareness of the importance of all aspects of health (physical, mental, and social) has led to a comprehensive view of physical education emphasizing development of a healthy body, mind, and spirit, together with a focus on the individual's role in contributing to the health of society in general. Thus, physical education teaches all children to enjoy being physically active to the extent that they are able, resolve conflicts peacefully, and prepare for a long, healthy, active life.

CHAPTER THREE

PHYSICAL EDUCATION
GUIDELINES
for
KINDERGARTEN
through
GRADE TWELVE

CHAPTER THREE

This chapter outlines the essential concepts, skills, and activities of a comprehensive physical education system for children in kindergarten through grade twelve. For each grade level the chapter presents the following elements:

- The primary emphasis of physical education for the grade level
- Background information on developmental appropriateness and readiness
- Actions and concepts to be highlighted in physical education instruction for each of the three goals of physical education
- Sample expectations for student performance[1] (Note that these are only examples of desired expectations and do not constitute a complete profile of expectations for the grade level. The expectations for students should be based on the previous curriculum offered and the students' previous experiences, including those of students with disabilities. See the section on students with disabilities in Chapter 5.)

Although developmental appropriateness figures importantly in these guidelines, instructors should be aware that students are likely to display some characteristics and skills appropriate to groups above and below their age-mates. Instructors should also be aware of a general progression from learning the basics to being a self-directed learner that all students are capable of experiencing.

---

[1] Some of the suggested expectations are adapted from *Outcomes of Quality Physical Education Programs* (Reston, Va.: National Association for Sport and Physical Education, 1992). The document can be ordered for $6 from the National Association for Sport and Physical Education, 1900 Association Dr., Reston, VA 22091-1599; telephone (703) 476-3410. Discounts are available for multiple copies.

At the elementary level the physical education curriculum needs to focus on basic skills by having students participate in many types of age-appropriate activities. As their skills develop, students can begin to understand that correct practice will result in improved learning and development of competency. In the upper elementary grades, students can become involved in activities that will assist in their own learning and help them begin to appreciate individual differences in their peers. At the middle school level, students can benefit from experiences that will assist them in evaluating and measuring their own performance. They can begin to recognize and develop practice schedules for different skills appropriate to their varying abilities. They can also be involved in activities in which they design schedules with and give appropriate feedback to their peers. Eventually, students can apply these concepts to new skills and thus transfer learning. At the high school level, students may design their own learning schedules based on their own choice of activities.

Throughout, it is important for planners and instructors to become aware of the total experience of a comprehensive system across age groups. Even during the early stages, a well-planned physical education program takes account of the long-term goals. Teachers of primary students are aware, for example, that students are moving toward the ultimate goal of making independent choices about physical activity in their teenage years. In addition, the element of pleasure in physical activity and an emphasis on pleasurable play should be a continual focus of physical education.

KINDERGARTEN

Emphasis: How I Move in My Environment

Background

Children at this stage are solo learners. They focus primarily on moving within space, including the general space around them and their own personal space. Nonlocomotor skills include how the body moves on its axis, and locomotor skills include moving in general space. Once the children are able to move effectively in their space, they focus on objects—for example, equipment, supplies, and materials. They also learn about and interpret their environment through play. They should move in a safe environment that helps them look forward to positive experiences in physical education.

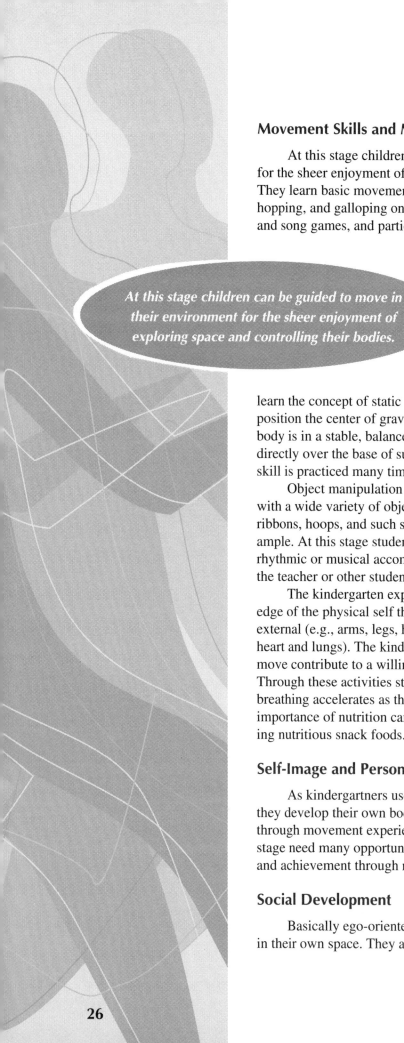

Movement Skills and Movement Knowledge

At this stage children can be guided to move in their environment for the sheer enjoyment of exploring space and controlling their bodies. They learn basic movement skills, including creeping, crawling, walking, hopping, and galloping on the preferred foot, playing rhythmic games and song games, and participating in circle or partner walks and marches. Nonlocomotor movement experiences include balancing, bending and stretching, twisting and turning, beating and shaking, tensing and relaxing, pushing and pulling, rising and falling, and participating in rhythmic and play activities that require those movements.

> *At this stage children can be guided to move in their environment for the sheer enjoyment of exploring space and controlling their bodies.*

Children in kindergarten also learn the concept of static stability by experiencing various balances that position the center of gravity over the base of support. They learn that the body is in a stable, balanced position when the center of gravity is directly over the base of support and that improvement occurs when a skill is practiced many times.

Object manipulation includes opportunities to manipulate and play with a wide variety of objects: lightweight balls, soft objects, beanbags, ribbons, hoops, and such student-made objects as sock balls, for example. At this stage students also perform free exploratory movement to rhythmic or musical accompaniment that is prerecorded or provided by the teacher or other students.

The kindergarten experience begins with the expansion of knowledge of the physical self through identification of body parts—both external (e.g., arms, legs, head, and facial features) and internal (e.g., heart and lungs). The kindergarten child's energy level and readiness to move contribute to a willingness to participate in aerobic-type activities. Through these activities students discover that the heart beats faster and breathing accelerates as they move their bodies. Learning about the importance of nutrition can begin at this level with instruction on selecting nutritious snack foods.

Self-Image and Personal Development

As kindergartners use their bodies to perform varied movements, they develop their own body image. Because self-image can be enhanced through movement experiences in physical education, children at this stage need many opportunities to experience personal feelings of success and achievement through movement.

Social Development

Basically ego-oriented, children in kindergarten tend to play alone in their own space. They are focused on themselves in the present.

However, they also begin to recognize the concept of self and others; acknowledge that others may occupy their space; learn to move about in their space without interfering with others; and begin to learn to take turns and share in interaction with others. Children at this stage generally do not understand the purpose of rules but will follow rules delivered by adults.

Sample Expectations

The student will be able to:

- Travel in different ways in a large group without bumping into others or falling.
- Balance while bending, twisting, or stretching.
- Strike a stationary ball with any part of the body.
- Identify various parts of the body and their location—for example, arms, legs, and hands.
- Recognize changes in heart rate.
- Follow adult-delivered rules.

GRADE ONE

Emphasis: Moving Through Space and Time

Background

Students at this stage expand their movement skills to include qualities of space and time by learning to move in different directions at varying speeds. They explore a variety of movements, such as high-low and fast-slow. They also learn to recognize the element of time in movement—for example, how long it takes to move from one place to another and how long it takes an object to travel from one place to another.

Movement Skills and Movement Knowledge

Through movement experiences first graders develop an awareness of the concepts of space, time, and effort. These experiences should include many opportunities for children to feel the joy that results from having the ability and freedom to explore, discover, and express themselves through movement.

As they continue motor learning, first graders accept challenges to move through space with the added dimensions of time and effort, such as fast-slow and strong-weak. Direction in movement is introduced along with basic eye-hand and eye-foot manipulative skills. Locomotor activities include hopping on the nonpreferred foot; galloping on the nonpreferred foot; and marching, sliding, and performing other patterns according to specific rhythms. Nonlocomotor movements include symmetrical and asymmetrical balances, lifting and carrying, starting and stopping, swinging, swaying, curling, and stationary dodging.

Students make deliberate moves in specified directions. They learn the biomechanical principle of dynamic stability. That is, balance is inherent in all movement, and individuals can increase their static stability by widening their base of support and lowering their center of gravity. They also learn that movement begins when their center of gravity moves to the edge of their base of support, their center of gravity is raised, and their base of support is narrowed. For example, a student is running, comes to a stop to maintain balance, and resumes running.

Balance is inherent in all movement.

Students begin to manipulate objects with purposeful movement and learn to roll, toss underhand, bounce with two hands, retrieve, stationary-kick, and strike with the hand various objects that are safe and nonthreatening. Simple dances in columns and circles and basic partner dances are appropriate at this level.

Although the child's movement becomes more purposeful and performance more deliberate, the instructor should encourage interest in the performance of an activity rather than any particular level of achievement. Especially at the beginning of the year, the physical education program should include familiar and enjoyable games and activities that allow for each child's full participation.

First graders learn about the body's need for oxygen and food as fuel to supply the body with energy. They also learn about the role of the circulatory system in moving oxygenated blood to the muscles. They reflect on how their bodies feel as they experiment with different types of movement—for example, differing periods of time and types of space. The relationship of nutrition and exercise to physical strength and energy should be introduced at this level.

Self-Image and Personal Development

Children at this stage begin to form a personal body image through comparison with others. They learn that the body undergoes marked changes in height and weight and that those changes influence the movement and coordination of body parts.

Social Development

First graders participate in parallel play with other students and tend to be more involved in individual activities than in interaction with others. They continue to learn in groups but participate as individuals.

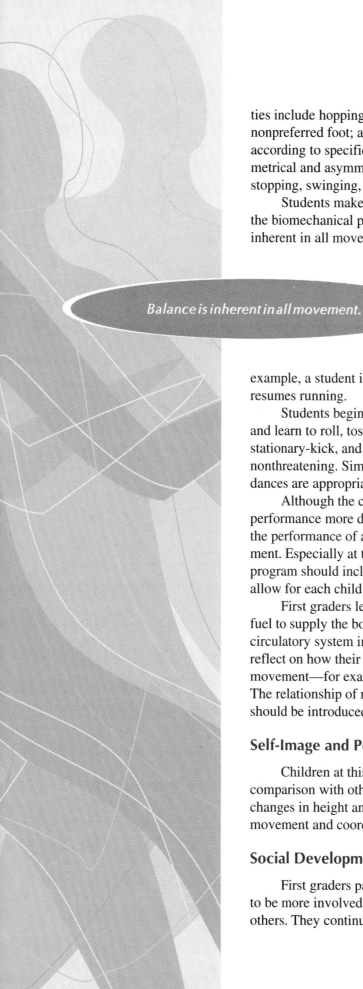

Multicultural experiences should be interwoven as appropriate—beginning in grade one and continuing through each level.

Sample Expectations

The student will be able to:

- Travel and change direction quickly in response to a signal.
- Travel in relationship to objects: over, under, behind, and through.
- Place the body and limbs in different positions, demonstrating high, middle, and low levels.
- Toss and catch a ball alone or with a partner.
- Learn to use equipment safely and responsibly.
- Begin to recognize changes in his or her body, such as changes in height and weight.
- Develop responsibility for expected behaviors on the playground and in the classroom.

GRADE TWO

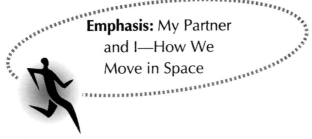

Emphasis: My Partner and I—How We Move in Space

Background

At this stage students explore movement patterns with a partner to define movement in relation to another person, shape, or group. They learn by continuing to experience a variety of modalities, including kinesthetic learning. Since the students are highly flexible in interacting with partners, activities should encourage changes of partners. In the application of rules, fairness at this stage is flexible, and children are likely to make up their own rules as they play together.

Movement Skills and Movement Knowledge

Total physical response—response with the entire body—occurs in motor movement as the student learns to define movement in relation to another person, shape, group, or group shape. Locomotor patterns include leaping and skipping, dancing with a partner, and dancing in a double circle. Nonlocomotor movements include dynamic balancing, dodging while moving, pantomiming, and mirror moving.

As students begin to play in partnerships, simple dances for couples, such as the Children's Polka, are appropriate. To understand movement and apply laws of motion at higher grade levels, students learn to describe movement and differentiate among speed, velocity, and acceleration. With partners second graders are able to compare various speeds and velocities. For example, students can talk about how fast they can run or walk and the difference between running and walking and other modes of locomotion.

Manipulative skills include catching a rolled ball; throwing and catching after one bounce (solo and with a partner); and kicking a stationary ball in a variety of ways. In addition to physical practice, students at this level should be encouraged to begin to use visualization and mental practice to reinforce learning.

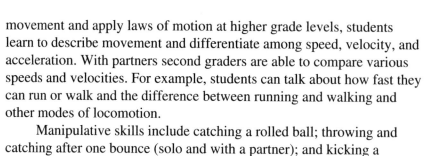

Fairness at this stage is flexible, and children are likely to make up their own rules as they play together,

The study of exercise physiology considers how the heart and lungs work as partners in cardiorespiratory health. In pairs students monitor the pulse at rest, during exercise, and after exercise. As they participate in movement that accelerates breathing and pulse rate, they learn the concept of the body's need for exercise to accelerate breathing and pulse rates on a regular basis. Nutrition, with a focus on foods healthy for the heart, is another factor in developing students' knowledge and skills related to cardiorespiratory health.

Self-Image and Personal Development

Growth rates vary during this stage. As the children's awareness of others increases, they are able increasingly to see themselves in relation to others. They are also able to recognize and appreciate their own positive and negative feelings and those of others.

Social Development

In grade two children learn more about relationships between themselves and others. They move from the sense of self in isolation and begin to embrace the concept of *we* and *partners*. This is also a time when children's growing awareness of others can help to promote knowledge of individual differences and different cultures. That can be the springboard, in turn, for encouraging children to accept and appreciate differences in others.

The children are able to celebrate the successes of others and begin to recognize specific activities that contribute to feelings of joy and movement experiences that rely on cooperation. They consistently practice sharing and caring skills when playing with partners in movement activities and reinforce one another by giving and receiving encouragement.

Sample Expectations

The student will be able to:

- Move backwards and change direction quickly and safely without falling.
- Jump and land, using a combination of one- and two-foot take-offs and landings.
- Throw a ball hard, demonstrating an overhand technique, a side orientation, and opposition.
- Jump a self-turned rope repeatedly.
- Skip, hop, gallop, and slide.

GRADE THREE

Emphasis: Continuity and Change in Movement

Background

Reacting and responding to others take precedence at this stage. By now students have a self-image strong enough to tolerate differences in how others react to them and are better able to make well-defined combinations of movements. Groups should never number more than five, the number that provides everyone with many turns and allows for natural leaders and followers to emerge.

Movement Skills and Movement Knowledge

Students' motor ability increases as they gain greater control. They begin to develop a concept of the order of a sequence in movement and willingly experiment with and explore alternative movements.

Third graders learn a variety of rhythmic patterns and grade-appropriate dances, using specific movement patterns, such as step-hop, step-swing, and two-step. Nonlocomotor skill development focuses on balance, including the use of apparatuses, inverted balances, balance on various body parts, and partner balances. Students are able to describe muscular movement as the internal force that causes the body to change from a stationary to a moving object. They can also describe gravity, friction, and muscular movements as the external forces that cause the body to stop. They learn that specific types of movement provide benefits not only in developing skills but also in developing and maintaining health fitness. Striking skills, such as dribbling and volleying, continue to be refined. Students are also able to discriminate among cues, adjust to cues, and determine appropriate movements for specific situations.

This stage foreshadows the marked physical changes that will take place in later childhood. The exercise physiology experience for grade three includes an emphasis on the importance of aerobic exercise for cardiorespiratory health, including the principles of warming up before exercising and cooling down afterward. In keeping with the grade-level emphasis on continuity and change, students participate in warm-up exercises to change the body to a readiness state for more vigorous exercise. In extended periods of aerobic activity, they also experience continuity of effort in cardiorespiratory conditioning. A third health-fitness component, flexibility, is emphasized during the warm-up and cooling-down phases.

Self-Image and Personal Development

Third graders begin to express themselves by creating new movement patterns involving time, space, and flow. They continue to celebrate successes and identify activities contributing to feelings of joy through active play.

Social Development

Students learn through play to handle individual responsibilities and resolve personal differences, becoming more capable of working together for a common goal as they grow in their ability to cooperate and take turns. The teacher should encourage the formation of groups of mixed gender during structured sessions because at this level boys and girls tend to separate for free play.

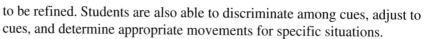

Groups should never number more than five, the number that provides everyone with many turns and allows for natural leaders and followers to emerge.

During this stage students begin to gain respect for other classmates and for the property of others, understand different types of play, and assist each other by practicing with a partner the rules of fair play. They learn to listen to each other and to react and respond appropriately.

Sample Expectations

The student will be able to:

- Combine locomotor and nonlocomotor movements, such as combining various travel patterns in relation to music.
- Dribble a ball continuously, using the hands or feet to control it.
- Maintain flexibility by combining shapes, levels, and pathways into simple sequences.
- Recognize similar movement concepts in a variety of skills. For example, an underhand movement can be used in a variety of ways.

- Accept the feelings resulting from challenge, success, and failure in physical activity.
- Play and assist others in activities in groups of three to five.

GRADE FOUR

Emphasis: Manipulating Objects in and Through Space

Background

Fourth graders are at a stage between childhood and youth during which they are growing in definite patterns. Eye-hand coordination is improved, and fine-motor activities are becoming more skillful. In addition, the greatest gain in strength begins at this stage. Students have mastered many locomotor and nonlocomotor skills and are able to manipulate objects in a variety of ways. They can create a game, for example, when they are given an object and encouraged to play. Physiologically, while they are standing, their center of gravity is still located in the midsection of the body, making balance and manipulation of objects a challenge. Fourth graders are likely to test rules during play and challenge how rules apply to them. Further, they tend to regard rules as rigid and prescriptive. When exceptions to the rules have to be made, the logic and rationale of the rules should be emphasized.

Movement Skills and Movement Knowledge

In motor development students at this level are able to focus on refining their skills in comparison with proficiency standards. They begin to use space and distance appropriately as they progress toward accuracy in throwing, catching, manipulating the body in space, and striking with body parts and objects—for example, volleying and dribbling a basketball with the hands and moving a soccer ball with the feet. They also learn about the concepts of projection—for example, applying greater force to an object to make it travel farther and knowing how to generate force by maintaining firm contact with the ground when the object is released.

Rhythmic activities include specific dances that may be related to the history–social science curriculum, such as dances appropriate to specific regions, ethnic groups, and cultures. Students also learn that there are many ways to learn and practice movement skills and that a practice session can be conducted in a variety of ways. Whole practice involves learning an entire sequence of movements that combine into a complex skill pattern; partial practice involves concentrating on one fundamental movement. Some skills may be introduced whole, learned in parts, and then practiced whole. Fitness-conditioning activities focus on various types of health-fitness exercises and many ways to combine those exercises into an exercise program.

Another focus is on how physical exercise conditions the heart, lungs, and muscles. Students learn to differentiate between aerobic exercises that provide cardiorespiratory benefits and those that do not. They also learn about the importance of muscular endurance and strength as components of fitness. The role of nutrients in forming body composition and providing the energy needed to sustain physical movement should also be emphasized.

Self-Image and Personal Development

At this level students are ready to cope with success and failure and are more perceptive and accepting of similarities and differences. This is also a time for developing, in the individual and in the group, wholesome attitudes toward victory and defeat.

Appreciation of different styles of movement and the uniqueness of movement in various cultures begins to occur. Thus, fourth graders appreciate a sense of personal uniqueness in movement and become aware of the similarities and differences between themselves and others.

Social Development

Fourth graders are ready to take the initiative within the group and demonstrate leadership as well as learn to be a good follower. This level is appropriate for the introduction of more complex games that challenge and increase performance abilities and enhance social skills.

Fourth graders are able to cooperate with a partner in using equipment and helping one another improve object manipulation skills.

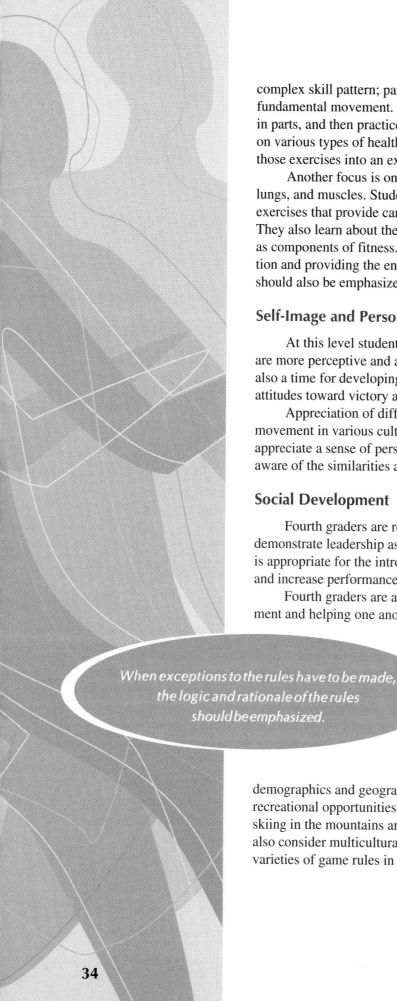

When exceptions to the rules have to be made, the logic and rationale of the rules should be emphasized.

Working together as part of large groups, they begin to appreciate personal differences and value the rights of others. They want to follow rules; thus, they need to learn to cope with conflicts and disputes by practicing conflict-resolution skills.

While considering diversity in California, students observe that local demographics and geography influence the type of physical activities and recreational opportunities available within a given area—for example, skiing in the mountains and swimming and surfing at the ocean. Students also consider multicultural influences on the evolution of games and the varieties of game rules in different geographical areas.

34

Sample Expectations

The student will be able to:

- Leap, leading with either foot.
- Hand-dribble and foot-dribble a ball while moving within a group.
- Jump and land for height and distance.
- Maintain continuous aerobic activity for a specified time.
- Describe healthful benefits that result from regular participation in physical activity.
- Recognize the fundamental strategies in simple games.

GRADE FIVE

Emphasis: Manipulating Objects with Accuracy and Speed

Background

At this level students continue to manipulate a variety of objects according to more specific goals. Now accuracy and speed, with a focus on targets, become important. Eye-hand, eye-foot, and other forms of coordination begin to come together. Fifth graders try continually to improve their motor skills, celebrate their successes and achievements, and take pride in individual excellence. Groups are expanded to include more than five students, and cooperative learning parallels that of other academic subjects. At this level the concept of fairness is emphasized. Students may be willing to change rules in order to achieve fairness for all.

Movement Skills and Movement Knowledge

At this stage specific body types are more efficient in certain movements, skills, and activities as body size and strength increase steadily. As students continue to improve in motor performance, they become more proficient in basic skills, such as running, jumping, and throwing. The ten-year-old begins to concentrate on the development of selective motor skills.

Fifth-grade students manipulate objects through space with accuracy and with the added element of speed. As they practice for skill and accuracy, students learn that the desired expectation determines the type of practice needed to achieve that goal. One type of practice may be to concentrate on improving speed, another on improving accuracy, and still another on improving both.

In the application of Newton's second law, students experiment in throwing different sizes of balls (golf ball, shot, softball), discovering that smaller objects will travel farther than heavier objects when the same amount of force is used. When speed is the objective, they learn to use a flat trajectory. They learn that to catch an object, they must increase (1) the distance through which the object moves after contact; or (2) the size of the area that absorbs the force of the object.

In grade five students examine the role of the circulatory system and its relationship to overall health. They are taught to develop strength and flexibility, including the interaction of strength and flexibility with the ability to perform forceful movements or manipulate objects with force. Further, they are taught how to maintain a healthy body by balancing food intake with physical activity (calories consumed and calories expended) and regulating the ratio of lean to fat body tissue.

Self-Image and Personal Development

Students at this stage learn to establish goals and select the practice techniques appropriate to the most immediate goals. They play gamelike activities in which the use of more than two skills to achieve objectives in the game is emphasized. Experiencing individual satisfaction increases at this stage as a motivational factor for future participation in a variety of activities. Increasingly, fifth-graders are able to use the body in movement to communicate feelings and to appreciate the aesthetic aspects of physical performance and the pleasure of achieving goals they have set for themselves.

Social Development

Fifth graders thrive in small-group activity in which three to five students interact in cooperative play. They assume increasingly complex roles in cooperative activities; begin to develop an awareness of individual differences related to gender, cultural heritage, ethnicity, and physical ability; and appreciate the positive aspects of diversity.

Social and game patterns include one against two, two against three, and two against two in activities such as goaltending. Students are beginning to recognize offensive and defensive play and understand that strategy is a skill to be developed within the context of play and games.

Fifth graders know how to apply rules and demonstrate a sense of fairness in games and activities. Contemporary music and dance are popular. The California Raisin Dance and the Electric Slide, for example, can be modified to create more complex dance patterns.

Sample Expectations

The student will be able to:

- Manipulate objects with accuracy and speed.
- Be involved in gamelike activities, with emphasis on more than two skills.

- Distinguish between compliance and noncompliance with game rules.
- Use fundamental strategies (i.e., offensive and defensive strategies) in simple games.
- Recognize that different body types are more effective in certain movement skills and activities.
- Begin to appreciate individual differences within small-group competition and cooperation.
- View the practice and perfection of performance in line and folk dances positively.

GRADE SIX

Emphasis: Working Cooperatively to Achieve a Common Goal

Background

Students at this stage are able to combine various skills in cooperative activities and give appropriate feedback to others. More independent in thought and action than younger students, they are also more likely to seek out new challenges in individual and group activities. Despite their desire for independence, however, sixth graders are likely to be genuinely interested in helping others. Because their interest in team play and organized games is strong, learning experiences can focus on developing the skills required for cooperative effort toward a common goal.

Movement Skills and Movement Knowledge

Students at this level are ready to combine skills for practice in lead-up games (a team, individual, or dual activity leading to an organized sport). These activities facilitate the learning of physical skills while allowing for cooperative effort. A unit should be included in sixth grade on cooperative games that can be used as lead-up games for more traditional sports. Juggling, unicycling, pogo-stick activities, bowling, foot-bag skill games, and throwing activities add variety and challenge as students improve their eye-hand and eye-foot coordination. This is also an appropriate time to add tumbling to previously learned stunts.

Students learn concepts related to Newton's third law. That is, when struck, an object will rebound in the opposite direction with the same amount of force with which it is hit. The harder an object is hit, the greater will be the force that causes the object to rebound in the opposite direction.

A child's development, which is influenced by heredity, hormones, nutrition, and exercise, is also influenced by cultural expectations and gender differences. Students should understand that the achievement of certain levels of physical skill is dependent on all of these factors and that they should accept individual differences.

Sixth graders are beginning to understand the purpose of each health-fitness component and the interrelatedness of all the fitness components in the development and maintenance of optimum health. Special emphasis should be given to the interaction of the circulatory and respiratory systems in conditioning for health fitness.

Self-Image and Personal Development

Students at this stage are able to recognize stylistic differences in performance, develop a more realistic self-image, and form collective attitudes as members of a group. They also begin to value looking good more than ever before as they become more aware of the varying levels of physical development within their peer group.

Despite the physiological differences that occur at this age, students are generally willing to work cooperatively toward a common goal because desire for recognition within the group is strong. The physical education experience should foster in each student a sense of acceptance and belonging and of being valued within the group or on a team.

Social Development

During lead-up games students at this level begin to recognize the validity of rule application and to accept that fairness applies to all. The grouping patterns for games can increase in size to six players. In keeping with the grade six history–social science focus on ancient civilizations, it is appropriate to introduce students to tribal dances and ethnic dances of contemporary or ancient cultures. Examples include the Pata Pata from South Africa, the Hora from Israel, and the High Life from Ghana.

Cooperation includes interacting with opponents in competitive activities to facilitate mutual development of skills.

As students work in cooperative groups, they learn to provide one another with feedback and support in skill execution. They learn through experimentation that specific, positive, corrective feedback improves skill development more rapidly than general, negative, or neutral feedback and that the more promptly feedback is given after performance, the more meaningful the feedback is.

Cooperation includes interacting with opponents in competitive activities to facilitate mutual development of skills. Sixth graders can accept and respect the performance of others, regardless of ability level, and are able to interact positively with others to develop friendships and participate in peer coaching activities with a partner.

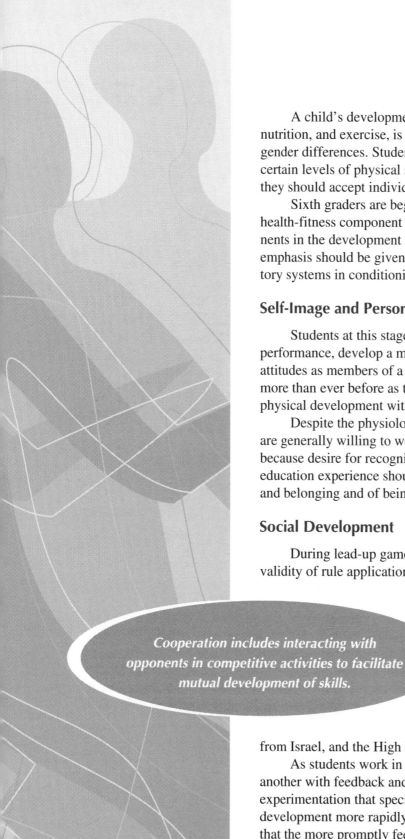

Sample Expectations

The student will be able to:

- Throw a variety of objects, demonstrating both accuracy and distance (e.g., disklike objects, deck tennis rings, footballs).
- Design and play small group games that involve cooperating with others to keep an object away from opponents (basic offensive and defensive strategy—for example, by throwing, kicking, or dribbling a ball).
- Design and refine a routine, combining various jump-rope movements to music, so that it can be repeated without error.
- Demonstrate correctly activities designed to improve and maintain muscular strength and endurance, flexibility, and cardiorespiratory functioning.
- Participate in games, sports, dance, and outdoor pursuits, both in and outside of school, according to individual interests and capabilities.
- Recognize the role of games, sports, and dance in getting to know and understand people of diverse cultures.

GRADE SEVEN

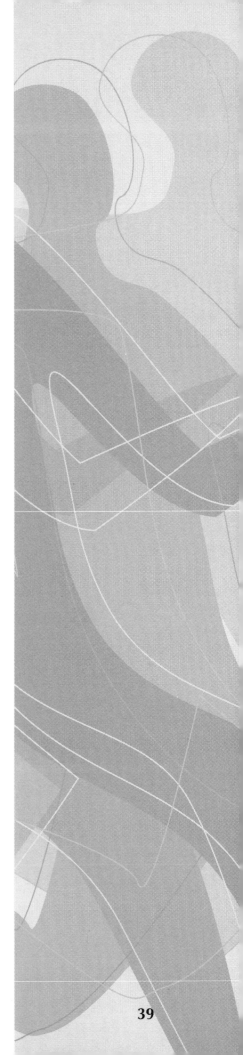

Emphasis: Meeting Challenges and Making Decisions

Background

A well-planned physical education program takes into account the importance of the transition from sixth to eighth grade and the rapid physical, social, and emotional changes occurring at this level. Students are beginning to look for a sense of belonging, community, peer group, and team even as they are gaining more confidence in individual activities. They have an eagerness to test themselves, both individually and in groups. This is an appropriate time to introduce individual risk taking and individual sports rather than focus exclusively on team sports.

Movement Skills and Movement Knowledge

Students at this stage tend to enjoy risk-related activities. Unless the school curriculum provides such activities in a safe environment, the students are likely to pursue the activities on their own without supervision. Appropriate activities include aquatics; combatives (e.g., self-defense and fencing); tumbling; gymnastics; individual and dual sports;

and outdoor education, such as adventure-based activities and orienteering. Specific adventure-based activities might include problem-solving exercises in which students work in small groups to solve physical challenges; trust falls (the student falls backward into the arms of partners); low-rope activities, such as balancing on a log suspended above the ground; high-rope activities in which students are involved in rappelling or rock climbing; and rollerskating, skateboarding, and cycling. The tumbling unit introduced in grade six can be extended at this level to include apparatus for gymnastics and rhythmic gymnastics.

A well-planned physical education program takes into account the importance of the transition from sixth to eight grade and the rapid physical, social, and emotional changes occurring at this level.

Seventh graders should learn more about the principles of spin and rebound. Spin results when force is applied off the center of an object. Students should become familiar with and begin to experiment with spins of various types: counterclockwise, clockwise, backspin, and topspin. They should learn how spin can be used to gain strategic advantage by players who understand how to apply it.

Dance should include folk dances and other dances from cultures around the world to help students develop greater understanding and acceptance of their own heritage and that of others.

As for motor learning, students at this level should understand that performance is measurable in terms of technique, accuracy, distance, and speed. They should be able to chart their own motor skill development in specific activities and events.

Seventh graders are also able to understand the interrelationship of the health-fitness components in the development of optimum health and thus to select specific exercises for each component. This is an appropriate time to introduce the *FIT* guidelines for physical exercise, which are the appropriate **f**requency, **i**ntensity, and **t**ime required for benefits to be accrued in each health-fitness component. Students should learn the principles of overload, progression, and specificity in physical conditioning.

Students' growth rates vary considerably during this period of development. Many experience their most rapid growth, and an increasing number show signs of puberty. All need to be aware that they must continue strenuous activity to maintain strength, speed, and endurance as their bodies change. They should study the impact of such factors as exercise, relaxation, nutrition, stress, and substance abuse on the body's ability to participate in physical exercise and on general well-being. Screening for posture deviation is required of all seventh graders, and parents must be notified when further examination is recommended.

Self-Image and Personal Development

The seventh grader is entering a time when he or she is more likely than ever before to take on new challenges, solve new problems, and be willing to take new risks. Risk taking involves new challenges and learning opportunities—trying out new equipment and new ways to use old equipment. Risk taking is attractive to students both alone and with others. They should be given a variety of opportunities to experience controlled risks through such activities as planned outdoor adventure activities and ropes courses. Students are also more likely to accept the challenge of setting personal goals for improvement related to health fitness and performance skills.

Social Development

Seventh graders are increasingly able to meet challenges, solve problems, and resolve conflicts within a group. They are more likely to express an appreciation for cooperation and fair play as they adhere to group rules. This is also a time when students develop confidence to overcome anxieties associated with attempting something new, making new friends, and beginning to accept their own limitations.

Sample Expectations

The student will be able to:

- Leap, roll, balance, transfer weight, bat, volley, hand- and foot-dribble, and strike a ball with a paddle, using mature motor patterns.
- Participate in vigorous activity for a sustained period of time while maintaining a target heart rate.
- Identify proper warm-up, conditioning, and cooling-down techniques and the reasons for using them.
- Describe ways to use the body and movement activities to communicate ideas and feelings.
- Accept and respect the decisions made by game officials—whether they are students, teachers, or officials outside of school.
- Become engaged in activities that provide for challenge, problem solving, decision making, and risk taking.

GRADE EIGHT

Emphasis: Working as a Team to Solve Problems

Background

At this stage students are able to focus on a common group or team goal over the long term, working together to solve problems during group activities. The emphasis in physical education moves toward team sports,

including defensive and offensive strategies. Students should be encouraged to continue participation in group activities because all aspects of the personal development of eighth graders, both physical and mental, are still evolving.

Movement Skills and Movement Knowledge

By the end of the eighth grade, students should have experienced a wide variety of activities. Now they can begin to see relationships among sports skills. For example, they may learn the underhand pitch for softball in one unit and transfer that skill to the underhand serve in volleyball and the serve in badminton. They should also be encouraged to understand that in certain situations transfer of learning can have a negative effect, such as learning the forehand drive in tennis and then applying it to the forehand drive in badminton.

A comparison of the offensive and defensive techniques used in team sports should be offered to help eighth graders learn the basic principles of strategy. In addition, students should have the opportunity to continue in a tumbling/gymnastics unit and a dance unit. Group dances, such as square, round, and contemporary line dances with directional changes requiring group cooperation, are appropriate.

In eighth grade students learn the principles of rotation. That is, to rotate an object, one must apply torque. They also learn that the closer the mass is to the axis, the greater the rotary velocity will be. Eighth graders have many opportunities to experiment with these concepts, particularly during the gymnastics unit.

Students learn that growth in height and weight alters the mechanical nature of performance and that motor performance is related to all measures of maturity (chronological, anatomical, and physiological).

Eighth graders are able to begin to design personal plans for a healthy life-style. Each student's plan should include exercises that take into account the FIT guidelines taught in grade seven and the principles of training. The importance of appropriate intensity in exercising should be emphasized as students learn to calculate their individual target heart rate for exercise and to understand the importance of cardiorespiratory conditioning. They should also be able to distinguish the health-related fitness components of cardiorespiratory endurance, muscular strength and endurance, flexibility, and body composition.

Self-Image and Personal Development

By eighth grade students should have developed skills needed to reduce stress. Their higher level of motor achievement provides a basis for establishing new personal goals that they can realistically attain.

Social Development

Students are able to accept responsibility for their behavior and resolve individual and group conflicts. They are mature enough to recognize the difference between ethical and unethical behavior and appreciate the importance of fair play, cooperation, and competition in team games, activities, and sports. They are also capable of playing on teams, making decisions, and solving problems associated with physical activities. Team games and team sports are of great interest and value to eighth graders of both genders because they help satisfy the students' need to feel a sense of belonging to a group.

The team-sports units should include the history, rules, and strategy of each sport. By this time students should understand that the rules are fair to all participants and allow for safe participation. They should also begin to generalize and understand that infringements of the rules involving other people are fouls; that infringements involving space, equipment, or time are violations; and that it is through the manipulation and understanding of the rules that strategies develop.

Group affiliation assumes added importance at this level, with emphasis being placed on team participation, roles of group members, group loyalty, and the identification of ethical and unethical behavior in group activities.

Group affiliation assumes added importance at this level, with emphasis being placed on team participation, roles of group members, group loyalty, and the identification of ethical and unethical behavior in group activities. Students begin to think of themselves as members of a team and learn to cooperate rather than dominate other team members in team and dual sports. They learn to identify and apply specific criteria for successful team participation and to lead and follow by sharing leadership positions.

Sample Expectations

The student will be able to:

- Explore introductory outdoor skills (e.g., backpacking, hiking, boating, cycling, ropes courses).
- Perform a variety of simple folk, country, and creative dances.
- Practice appropriate ways of learning new skills or sports on his or her own.
- Improve and maintain appropriate body composition.
- Describe long-term physiological, psychological, and other benefits that may result from regular participation in physical activity.
- Recognize in playing team sports that rules are fair to all and allow for safe participation.
- Understand how growth in height and weight influences the mechanical nature of performance in physical activities.

Emphasis: Developing a Personalized Fitness Program for a Healthy Life-Style

Background

This is a stage at which students are able to synthesize much of what they have learned in the earlier grades, including knowledge of human growth, development, and physiology. Individuals are able to coalesce as a team and focus on the needs and contributions of other team members beyond themselves. Affiliation, a feeling of being connected and involved, is of primary importance to ninth graders. Students develop a willingness to acknowledge and respect stylistic differences in performance. The ninth-grade physical education program should encourage students to gain an appreciation of others' achievements, no matter how large or small, and to expand their ability to adapt to the needs of the group and demonstrate fairness toward all.

Movement Skills and Movement Knowledge

The major emphases of study in the ninth grade are fitness, team sports, gymnastics, and aquatics. In learning about fitness, the students become familiar with new concepts related to the physiology of exercise; become knowledgeable consumers in relation to fitness; and experience a wide variety of exercises for flexibility, muscular strength and endurance, and cardiorespiratory endurance. In team sports ninth graders should be encouraged to select a sport in which to specialize; learn the history, rules, and strategies of the sport; and become proficient in the appropriate skills. The gymnastics unit should be an extension of the earlier tumbling and gymnastics classes. Here, too, students should be encouraged to select an event in which to specialize.

For those students who already demonstrate proficiency in swimming, classes in water polo, skin diving, or advanced swimming can be offered. During an aquatics unit the students should learn the biomechanical principle of buoyancy. That is, to move efficiently through water, they must streamline their bodies to reduce the effect of drag. In addition, the swimmer's size, shape, surface, and speed of movement are factors affecting performance in swimming.

In grade nine the student is expected to develop an in-depth understanding of the components of total health fitness in a unit that emphasizes the physiological, psychological, and social benefits of a healthy, active life-style.

Students should also begin to identify preferences for types of physical activity that can be pursued over the long term for fitness and recreation, including individual, dual, or team sports. Ninth graders should be able to explain the social, personal, and health benefits of developing skills in sports, games, and dance. They should be able to describe the aesthetic qualities of movement; feel good as they move efficiently and effectively; and develop the ability to evaluate personal needs, interests, and capacities that contribute to their movement choices.

Self-Image and Personal Development

In physical education experiences the ninth grader should demonstrate patterns of behavior that reflect sound mental and emotional health, positive self-image, and acceptance of the total self. To help students achieve self-realization through physical activity, the physical education instructor should guide the student's choice of fitness programs and activities to ensure a healthy life-style throughout life. Each student should set personal goals for health and fitness, including goals for improving health through physical exercise.

Social Development

Ninth graders have the capacity to demonstrate mature teamwork by successfully resolving conflicts within the group. They should learn to cooperate in teamwork and in competition, analyze situations, find solutions to problems, obey rules, work for delayed rewards, and persevere toward a goal.

The ninth grader is becoming increasingly more interested in sports as both participant and spectator. This increased interest is associated with several factors in addition to physical conditioning. For example, students have more choices in transportation and consumer spending. And they are bombarded with advertisements for all types of participant and spectator sports.

The major emphases of study in the ninth grade are fitness, team sports, gymnastics, and aquatics.

Sample Expectations

The student will be able to:

- Analyze offensive and defensive strategies in games and sports.
- Participate in an individualized fitness program.
- Identify and follow rules while playing sports and games.
- Identify ways in which rules are more alike than different and describe the difference between violations and fouls.

Emphasis: Analyzing Skills for Effective Movement

Background

Students at this stage are capable of choosing the physical activities they want to pursue. They are more able to generalize from previous experiences and to apply biomechanical principles to the analysis of a variety of movement skills. A well-planned physical education program will offer students a wide variety of opportunities. It will focus on individual or team sports of choice, dance, and personal defense, among other activities.

Movement Skills and Movement Knowledge

The five emphases of study for the tenth grade are individual and dual sports, outdoor education, combatives, dance, and analysis of movement. The individual or dual sport may be of the student's own choosing and may include such outdoor activities as orienteering, rock climbing, backpacking, and skiing. A personal defense class meets the combatives requirement and teaches students to avoid dangerous situations while preparing to defend themselves. The dance unit can be an extension of units taught at earlier grade levels. It can also be an elective that allows students to specialize in a specific type of dance at an intermediate or advanced level.

The analysis-of-movement class should conclude grade ten whenever possible. Reviewing what they have learned throughout the kindergarten through grade ten physical education curriculum, students should explore the reasons for physical education being taught in school, including the relationship between physical education and personal and social development. This class should also prepare students to be informed consumers in physical and recreational activities they plan to pursue outside of school. By the end of this unit, students should have developed a lifetime plan for physical fitness and activity.

At this grade level students demonstrate improved performance, in part because their perceptual feedback has improved. They have acquired skills that are basic to efficient movement. In addition, they should have acquired a high level of physical fitness. They should be able to analyze the physiological and mechanical principles involved in human movement and make adjustments in physical exercise to achieve personal goals for fitness or motor performance or both.

The application of the principles of levers to movement should be introduced in tenth grade. The human skeletal system is made up primarily of third-class levers. Because the force arm (muscle) for human beings cannot be lengthened, the students should learn that in order to increase the force at impact with an object, they must strengthen the muscle or lengthen the striking element to increase the force. Students can apply these concepts in activities such as golf (by using a longer shaft when driving) and tennis (by straightening the arm at the moment of impact in the serve).

Self-Image and Personal Development

The awareness tenth graders have of the importance of commitment and dedication in physical education contributes to their desire to pursue excellence in a variety of ways—socially, emotionally, and intellectually. The tenth-grade physical education curriculum should emphasize that while learning any new skill, individuals go through three stages of learning: (1) the cognitive phase; (2) the practice phase; and (3) the automatic phase, in which skills can be performed without concentrated attention. Although moving through this cycle takes time, students at the high school level are mature enough to reach the automatic phase in selected skills.

Tenth-grade students should be encouraged to evaluate the potential benefits and risks of available exercise programs in the school and the community and the cost-effectiveness of exercise programs offered to students as consumers. Each student should plan a personal exercise program that is physiologically sound and appropriate to his or her needs, interests, level of ability, and goals for health fitness.

Social Development

Tenth graders are often ready to assume leadership roles. By serving as peer coaches, they can take the initiative to assist other students by analyzing their application of the principles of biomechanics and by providing feedback and suggestions for improvement. As they become more concerned with social etiquette, they can study the ways in which society's rules are expressed through games and sports. In addition, they can develop an awareness of the ways in which society influences their choice of lifestyle as to types of physical activity and the degree of their participation in physical activity in and out of school. Students at this level also develop an appreciation of movement as an art form that reflects cultural values.

> *As students become more concerned with social etiquette, they can study the ways in which society's rules are expressed through games and sports.*

Sample Expectations

The student will be able to:

- Demonstrate basic competence in physical activities selected from each of the following categories: aquatics; self-defense; dance; individual, dual, and team activities and sports; and outdoor pursuits.
- Perform a variety of dances (folk, country, social, and creative) with fluency and in time to accompaniment.
- Use biomechanical concepts and principles to analyze and improve performance of self and others.
- Discuss the importance of balanced nutrition for a maintaining a healthy life-style.
- Design and implement a personal fitness program that relates to total wellness.
- Participate in a variety of game, sport, and dance activities representing different cultural backgrounds.
- Discuss the historical roles of games, sports, and dance in the cultural life of a population.
- Acknowledge and respect stylistic differences in performance.

GRADES ELEVEN AND TWELVE

Emphasis: Selecting Activities for the Pursuit of Individual Excellence

Background

Students at this level continue to specialize in activities of their own choosing. In addition, they can pursue excellence in the activities they choose, following a specific regimen and honing specific skills. They are able to develop a personalized plan for lifetime fitness by assessing personal needs, interests, abilities, and opportunities in the area of fitness and by selecting activities that contribute to the achievement of personal fitness goals. They can also focus on combatives; outdoor education; aquatics; team sports and individual and dual sports of choice; tumbling; gymnastics; and dance. They can apply knowledge, skills, and attitudes acquired in physical education experiences from kindergarten through grade twelve to become proficient in one or more activities that lead to achieving personal goals for lifetime fitness. Schools should be encouraged to be creative in developing their physical education electives for these grade levels.

Movement Skills and Movement Knowledge

By the eleventh and twelfth grades, students are prepared to focus on the activities they plan to pursue after graduation from high school. They are able to explain why an individual's pursuit of excellence in any arena is an evolving process requiring commitment, courage, confidence, initiative, and perseverance. They have learned that self-expression through physical activity is of great value in developing and maintaining the healthy mind and body needed to excel in life. Students should be encouraged to select a variety of activities that correspond to their personal needs, interests, and capacities. They should also be encouraged to reassess their changing needs and interests continually as they grow and mature.

An individual's pursuit of excellence in any arena is an evolving process requiring commitment, courage, confidence, initiative, and perseverance.

Students should be encouraged to select activities in which they will continue to specialize. Therefore, the biomechanical principles they study should be directly related to the activities they select. The students should also be encouraged to apply their knowledge of exercise physiology in planning and pursuing life-styles conducive to maintaining optimum health.

Self-Image and Personal Development

The senior high school student is at a stage where he or she can develop an increased interest in selecting activities in accordance with personal body type and capacities. By the eleventh grade students should have learned to evaluate personal performance in a variety of activities. They should be given the opportunity for self-direction in the selection of activities that can be enjoyed for health and fitness throughout life. Having selected activities for specialization, the student should have the motivation to learn. Students should be aware that the learning process takes them through three stages of learning (see "Grade Ten") and should understand that they must repeat and practice skills in a variety of ways in order to achieve excellence. They should also know how to measure their performance at different stages to maintain their motivation and adjust their goals for future training.

By the eleventh and twelfth grades, students are prepared to focus on the activities they plan to pursue for recreation or a career after graduation from high school. Elective units in a wide range of activities should last for a sufficient period of time. Students who complete these classes should be well prepared to continue the activity on their own.

Social Development

Students should be encouraged to work in small groups to provide one another with specific positive/corrective feedback so that individual excellence can be achieved. They should apply social skills acquired in physical education activities in preschool through grade twelve to enhance their own experience and the experience of others with whom they are involved in physical and social activities. They should also be encouraged to support and participate in community organizations that promote health and fitness by providing lifelong recreational opportunities for people of all ages.

Sample Expectations

The student will be able to:

Grade eleven:

- Use the principles of movement to accomplish a task with the least effort.
- Demonstrate some mastery of skills in games, sports, and dances and participate in intramural programs.
- Comprehend the correct elements of various movements, strategies, safety procedures, and basic rules.
- Show evidence of developing and maintaining physical fitness to achieve the goal of a healthy life-style.
- Show evidence of a positive self-image.
- Share in the responsibility of group action and problem solving as a member of a group or team.

Grade twelve:

- Excel and continue in an activity of choice, such as a sport, dance, gymnastics, or aquatics.
- Demonstrate advanced competence in at least one activity from the curriculum.
- Be able to design and execute a physical fitness program, recognizing that changes in life-style may progress over time from vigorous activities to mild exercise, including walking.
- Accept the ways in which personal characteristics, performance styles, and activity preferences will change over the life cycle.
- Know about career opportunities in physical education and related fields.
- Evaluate critically the claims made in advertisements about commercial products and programs.

CHAPTER FOUR

ENVIRONMENT NEEDED
for a
QUALITY
PHYSICAL EDUCATION
PROGRAM

CHAPTER FOUR

A positive, supportive environment is important to the success of the overall physical education program. Support for physical education should include the following elements:

- Physical education is recognized as an integral part of the school curriculum.
- Physical education continually supports and interacts with other subject areas.
- Physical education is included as part of a planned staff development program.
- Facilities, equipment, and supplies are provided that are safe and adequate.
- The psychological environment enables and encourages all students to succeed in physical education.
- The physical education program involves the school, the home, and the community.

Integral Part of the School Curriculum

As an integral part of the school curriculum, physical education should be taught by qualified professionals who have been trained in physical education or who have participated in a program of professional development focusing on the teaching of physical education. Classes for children and youths with special needs or disabilities should be taught by physical education teachers who know how to design and implement programs for such students. A quality physical education program provides equal access for all students and guarantees opportunities for maximum participation, optimum development, and appropriate individual attention. Opportunities for personal attention, individualized instruction, and time on task should be included.

Physical education teachers should be encouraged to participate on school or district interdisciplinary teams to develop the physical education curriculum. In a well-planned program the physical education teacher assumes responsibility for (1) implementing the physical education curriculum; (2) relating physical education to other subject areas; (3) working with other professionals to create interdisciplinary approaches to learning; and (4) promoting the cooperation of school, home, and community in providing the highest-quality physical education experience possible for every student.

Integration with Other Subject Areas

Physical education should continually support and interact with the other subject areas. For example, in its emphasis on personal health and the need for a healthy life-style, physical education reinforces but does not supplant health education. Teachers of physical education and health education should work together to integrate their curricula to reinforce the importance of maintaining an active and healthy life-style. Both can emphasize skills related to refusing negative pressures and influences, resolving conflicts, and coping with pressure, all of which are necessary for positive social interaction and healthy development.

Physical education classes provide a natural environment for the development of personal and social skills transferable to other situations and learning in other subject areas. There is a natural correlation, for example, between cooperative learning activities related to understanding the place of rules and strategies in physical education and the teaching of civic values, rights, and responsibilities in history–social science.

Continual interaction should occur between teachers of physical education and the rest of the staff. Through this interaction physical education and the other disciplines support and reinforce one other. Other examples of integration with the rest of the curriculum include the following:

> *Physical education classes provide a natural environment for the development of personal and social skills transferable to other situations and learning in other subject areas.*

- *Natural sciences*—through concepts related to gravity, levers, motion, physics, anatomy, biomechanics, and exercise physiology
- *Home economics*—through the study of exercise physiology and nutrition
- *History–social science*—through an emphasis on guiding students to become active, productive members of a democratic society; work cooperatively in groups and teams; and develop an understanding of

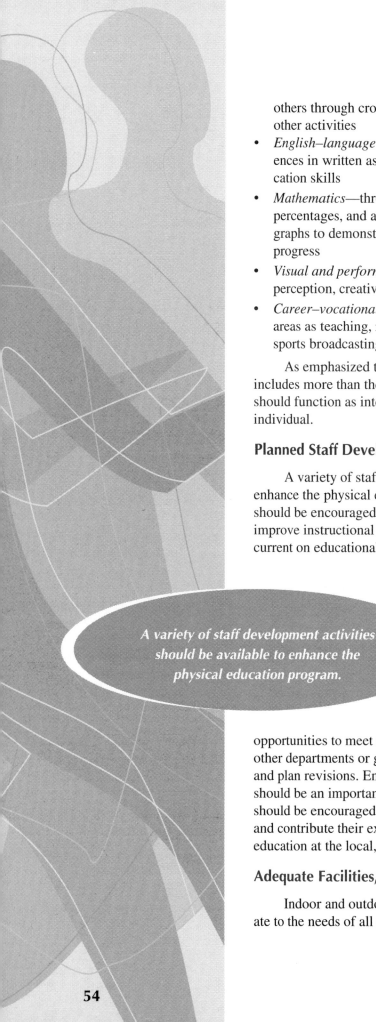

others through cross-cultural and multicultural games, dances, and other activities

- *English–language arts*—through applying physical education experiences in written assignments and other activities requiring communication skills
- *Mathematics*—through recording results and calculating probabilities, percentages, and averages related to physical activity or creating graphs to demonstrate measurements and comparisons of personal progress
- *Visual and performing arts*—through a shared emphasis on aesthetic perception, creative expression, rhythm, tempo, and meter
- *Career–vocational education*—through the study of careers in such areas as teaching, recreation, health, fitness, dance performance, and sports broadcasting

As emphasized throughout this framework, physical education includes more than the education of the physical body. All subject areas should function as integrated components in the education of the total individual.

Planned Staff Development Program

A variety of staff development activities should be available to enhance the physical education program. Teachers of physical education should be encouraged to (1) participate in ongoing staff development to improve instructional strategies and program implementation; (2) remain current on educational research; (3) learn to be effective with an increasingly diverse student population; and (4) enjoy the benefits of working and learning with other professionals in the field. They should also be encouraged to work with local colleges or universities to influence preservice training and provide in-service training opportunities.

> *A variety of staff development activities should be available to enhance the physical education program.*

At the school level physical education teachers should have opportunities to meet regularly with each other and with members of other departments or grade levels to assess the effectiveness of programs and plan revisions. Ensuring compliance with state and federal mandates should be an important part of the assessment process as well. Teachers should be encouraged to become involved in professional organizations and contribute their expertise to staff development projects in physical education at the local, state, and national levels.

Adequate Facilities, Equipment, and Supplies

Indoor and outdoor facilities must be sufficient in number, appropriate to the needs of all students, and accessible to the disabled. Dressing rooms must be clean and safe, adequate for the number of students served, and appropriately supervised without requiring physical education instructors to lose instructional time because of supervision. Equipment and supplies should be sufficient in quantity and quality to provide all students with opportunities to enjoy maximum participation.

Safety is an important priority in the environment for a quality physical education program. Staff members must be aware of safety concerns, protect students from unsafe equipment or facilities, and expect students to ensure their own safety and that of others. A student's lack of proficiency in English should not influence this priority in any way. Provisions should be made to ensure that all limited-English-proficient students understand rules and expectations regarding safety. Others to be considered in ensuring the safety of all students should be persons with disabilities.

Appropriate Psychological Environment

An appropriate environment for a quality physical education program enables and encourages all students to discover new concepts, skills, and abilities through movement experiences and other aspects of the physical education program. The atmosphere should be a nonthreatening one in which every student feels that to risk trying something new is safe physically, emotionally, and socially. Emphasis should be placed throughout on the development of movement skills, fitness and wellness, self-confidence, and social skills.

The atmosphere should be a nonthreatening one in which every student feels that to risk trying something new is safe physically, emotionally, and socially.

Because of the complexities of human growth and development and individual and cultural differences among students, a comprehensive physical education program should include a wide variety of movement experiences and teaching-learning strategies. All students should have the opportunity to be successful. Throughout, the student must experience a climate of respect—for oneself, for others, and for physical education generally, especially when students are being directed in attempts to refine skills or are being disciplined. Disciplinary procedures should be appropriate to the infraction, and the assignment of physical exercise should not be used as punishment. To do so will not instill in the student a love of physical activity.

Another important aspect of the psychological environment is an emphasis on accepting and celebrating ethnic and cultural diversity, one of the most challenging issues in education. Physical education offers unique opportunities to bring students together in nonthreatening ways that emphasize fairness and cooperation. Because physical education involves students in working and playing together, students must be

taught the personal and social skills, values, and attitudes needed for effective, positive social interaction. Disparaging remarks about an individual's disabilities, ethnicity, gender, native language, race, religion, or sexual orientation should not be tolerated. The physical education program must comply fully with all federal and state mandates.

Appropriate instruction in physical education for culturally diverse populations may require special teaching skills and a focus on students' unique needs. Teachers must avoid cultural or gender biases and refrain from stereotyping students. Students from different cultures may respond differently to directions from the teacher, praise and acknowledgment from others, perceived expectations, and physical interaction. Teachers should learn to recognize and understand the influence of their students' cultural heritage and learn to accommodate diversity while achieving the goals of the physical education curriculum.

Cooperation of School, Home, and Community

Although the school is the primary learning environment for physical education, the home and community also play significant roles. Only through the cooperation of the school, the home, and the community can students become fully prepared for lifelong participation in physical activity and effective social interaction.

The school site can become a focus for cooperation among families and outside support systems. Designating the school as the contact point provides families with more opportunities to receive services that benefit the child's health and development. For example, interaction of school and family can help to promote an acceptance of physically active and healthier, happier, more productive life-styles throughout the community. Schools can establish centers for wellness that provide assessment of physical well-being, individual counseling, and a variety of fitness activities. They can also involve families in other extracurricular activities at the school site and coordinate school and community recreational programs.

The community, working closely with the school, can play an active role in promoting fitness and wellness by providing opportunities for physical activity for families and individuals. Through participation in a variety of physical activities at school, students will be better prepared to take advantage of opportunities for physical activity provided in the home or in the community.

CHAPTER FIVE

QUALITY INSTRUCTION

in

PHYSICAL

EDUCATION

This framework describes a comprehensive physical education system that will prepare young people for a lifelong commitment to physical activity, health, and well-being. To achieve this end, however, all students must be given sufficient opportunities to accomplish the physical education learning goals for each grade level. What is required is a comprehensive physical education system of high quality and consistency throughout the grade levels. Most important, it implies quality instruction and positive, productive interactions between teachers and students.

To create high expectations for quality instruction, physical education teachers must continually strive to improve their effectiveness. This chapter offers a variety of approaches that can contribute to the overall success of physical education and enhance instructional quality and effectiveness.

Model Lesson

Teachers create an optimal learning environment and an effective learning experience for their students through careful planning. The heart of effective instruction is the actual physical education lesson.

Throughout the lesson the teacher should maintain an orderly, safe, businesslike atmosphere and have clear expectations for the behavior and achievement of students. The teacher implements the lesson plan and makes adjustments as necessary for students not experiencing success or not participating.

Each day should begin with a variety of *warm-up exercises* involving the muscles to be used in the instructional phase and lasting one or two minutes. All students should be expected to perform the exercises to the best of their ability. However, adjustments may need to be made to deal with individual abilities. The teacher supervises the students, explains the purpose of each exercise, and provides corrective or positive feedback.

Warm-up is followed by the *instructional phase.* At this point the teacher explains the purpose of the main activity, which will include demonstrations and explanations. Then comes the *activity phase.* During the activity phase each student is engaged in skill-learning time, with enough correct practice trials being provided during class time to acquire the desired skill. Activities should be designed to keep to a minimum the amount of time spent waiting in line and moving between activities. Equipment should be deployed efficiently (at least one object for every two students). Whenever possible, students should be placed in cooperative learning groups.

When working with individual students, the teacher should personalize instruction by using the student's name and giving feedback equally to boys and girls and to high achievers and low achievers in appropriate ways. At the end of the class, the teacher should provide a chance for *discussion or processing* of the lesson, encouraging the students to review the objectives or key points. In this way students can see relationships, attitudes, values, and other insights related to the lesson, and teachers can adjust the lessons for optimal learning the next day.

Components of a Model Physical Education Lesson

- Warm-up exercises
- Instructional phase
- Activity phase
- Discussion or processing

Variety of Strategies

Teachers should use a variety of teaching styles, including teacher-directed and student-initiated learning, to satisfy the learning styles of

individual students and stimulate higher levels of thinking and creativity. Teaching styles might include command, practice, self-check, guided discovery, student-designed and student-initiated teaching, and self-teaching. Teachers should also employ a variety of instructional approaches, including competency-based learning, contract learning, drill, information processing, lecture, mastery learning, programmed instruction, and role-playing.

Especially appropriate for physical education instruction is cooperative learning. Assigning students to small learning groups (three to six members each) allows teachers and students to achieve a variety of goals, both social and cognitive. In addition, research has shown that cooperative learning produces higher achievement; improves cross-ethnic friendships and social skills; enhances self-image; and promotes greater interdependence, improved role-taking abilities (e.g., leadership), and a better classroom climate.

The first step in cooperative learning is the formation of heterogeneous teams. The size of each team will vary according to the activity; however, groups of three to six students (mixed as to ability, race, and gender) have proven to be most successful. After the teams have been formed, students need activities for team building and time to practice and receive feedback on appropriate social skills.

The specifics of cooperative learning lessons depend to a great extent on which method among many different cooperative learning approaches is chosen. However, the teacher must ensure positive interdependence and both individual and group rewards. A team can succeed only if all members are interdependent in their contributions toward a common goal.

Instructional Media and Resources

Many types of instructional media and resources, as distinct from equipment for games and sports, are available to aid the physical education teacher. In addition to textbooks, workbooks, and more conventional printed materials, resources include films, filmstrips, videos, laser discs, CD-Rom, and large-screen projections of televised or videotaped images. Physical education teachers should look for ways not only to incorporate a variety of instructional media into their teaching but also to make sure that the media are available and are included in the overall budget for physical education.

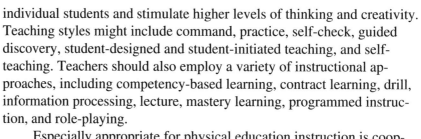
Examples abound of appropriate instructional technology in physical education.

Examples abound of appropriate instructional technology in physical education. Heart monitors can provide students with feedback on their heart rate while they are performing cardiovascular exercises. In addition, camcorders and video cameras can be used to capture students' performances for skill or strategy analysis. Computers can aid the teacher in the production of task cards or skill cards and can also be used to provide information and instructional modules to individuals or groups. When connected to laser disc players, videocassette players and other peripheral devices can capture students' interest through multimedia presentations.

A wide variety of computer software programs are available that lead students through tutorials on various sport or fitness concepts, offering both instruction and assessment procedures. An interactive laser-disc system can present students with information generated by computer software linked to the laser-disc player at different points in the tutorial. The player, instructed by the computer software, displays the appropriate live-action example. Interactive programs offer students a considerable amount of control over their own learning and the topics they wish to explore. Technology is also very useful in the assessment process.

Instructional Strategies to Meet Special Needs

Every physical education class includes students who are high achievers; those who are low achievers; and those, the majority, in the middle. Effective instructional strategies take into account the diverse needs of what are often very heterogeneous groups. All students, not just a select few, should receive positive feedback and reinforcement from the instructor or other students; and all should have opportunities to be involved.

All students, not just a select few, should receive positive feedback and reinforcement from the instructor or other students; and all should have opportunities to be involved.

Gender Equity

Federal law and California law require that students of both sexes be treated equally in integrated physical education classes. All students, male and female, should be given the teacher's attention and feedback on an equal basis and should be called on equally to demonstrate new skills. The teacher should also discipline males and females equally.

Students with Disabilities

Some students will come to physical education with motor or perceptual deficits; others, with more severe disabilities. Successful participation in physical activities by students with disabilities depends on the teacher's attitude and skill in providing instruction and support to all students. The teacher should continually encourage all students to learn and experience maximum enjoyment in physical education by understanding students' specific needs and encouraging students who are not disabled to accept and support those who are.

Children with disabilities, whether they are identified as needing special education and related services or not, have the right to a modification of the regular program. Further, under Section 504 of the Rehabilitation Act of 1973, Amendments of 1991 (Public Law 102–42), and the American with Disabilities Act of 1990 (Public Law 101–336), such children may not be discriminated against by school personnel. Service delivery options that must be made available to all children with disabilities are modified general physical education, specially designed physical education, and adapted physical education; direct services; collaboration; and consultation. For further information on adapted physical education program services, see Appendix B, "Program Advisory Clarifying Adapted Physical Education Program Services."

The teacher should continually encourage all students to learn and experience maximum enjoyment in physical education by understanding students' specific needs and encouraging students who are not disabled to accept and support those who are.

In some instances an individualized education program team at the school (e.g., the physical education teacher, the adapted physical education specialist, special education teachers, administrators, parents, and ancillary personnel, such as occupational therapists and physical therapists) will determine that the appropriate least-restrictive environment for a physical education program for students with disabilities is the general education class. To accommodate such students, the physical education instructor may have to make modifications and interventions.

In collaboration with the adapted physical education specialist, special education teachers, and ancillary personnel, the physical education teacher can modify instruction to accommodate students with disabilities without diminishing the value of the class for those without disabilities. Problem-solving skills and modified approaches to movement can be offered at the elementary level; flexible or optional unit schedules, at the middle or junior high school level; and elective or selective programs, at the senior high school level.

Teaching methods can be adapted to meet the needs of students through provision of a direct tutor, a buddy system that pairs students with disabilities with other students, peer tutoring, task cards or individualized learning packets, circuit or station setups, contracts or independent student programs, and other approaches. Other adaptations might include:

- Basing evaluation on the student's potential and on pretest and posttest comparison rather than on standardized scores
- Basing measurement on what the student with disabilities is able to

do rather than on what the student is not able to do

- Applying decathlon-scoring approaches to enable students with disabilities to compete for points against records that are appropriate to their physical status
- Providing specific devices or adapting equipment to aid in the manipulation of objects or oneself
- Using a larger ball or larger pieces of equipment to make the activity easier or to slow the pace of the activity
- Using a smaller, lighter ball or striking implement (plastic or soft ball or plastic bats) or an object that is easier to handle (beanbag or softball)
- Adding more players to a team to reduce the amount of activity and responsibility of any individual player
- Assigning playing positions according to the abilities of the students with disabilities
- Permitting the substitution or interchange of duties during participation
- Limiting play areas if students' movement capabilities are restricted

The physical education teacher should seek out opportunities for informal talks with the adapted physical education specialist or special education teacher to develop methods for working with students with disabilities. When these students cannot participate safely and successfully in the physical education program and when interventions have been ineffective, the specialist in adapted physical education must take a more active role. Use of the individualized education plan process for special education may be required.

Differences in Language or Communication

Different types of instructional approaches will also be needed for students with limited proficiency in English or other communication problems. Bilingual interpreters or instructors skilled in sign language may be needed. For non-English speakers, information offered in their native language helps develop not just understanding but a positive attitude toward the information.

For teachers who do not speak a second language and for students who are limited-English proficient, sheltered instruction is another approach that can be used. Sheltered instruction provides students with a variety of interactive and multimodal means to accessing information. In sheltered instruction the language demands of the lesson can be modified through such techniques as clear enunciation, controlled vocabulary, fewer idioms, and such contextual cues as gestures, facial expressions, demonstrations, props, visuals, and overhead transparencies. Cooperative learning has also proved effective in teaching students at various levels of English proficiency because high levels of interaction are associated with enhanced learning of content and English.

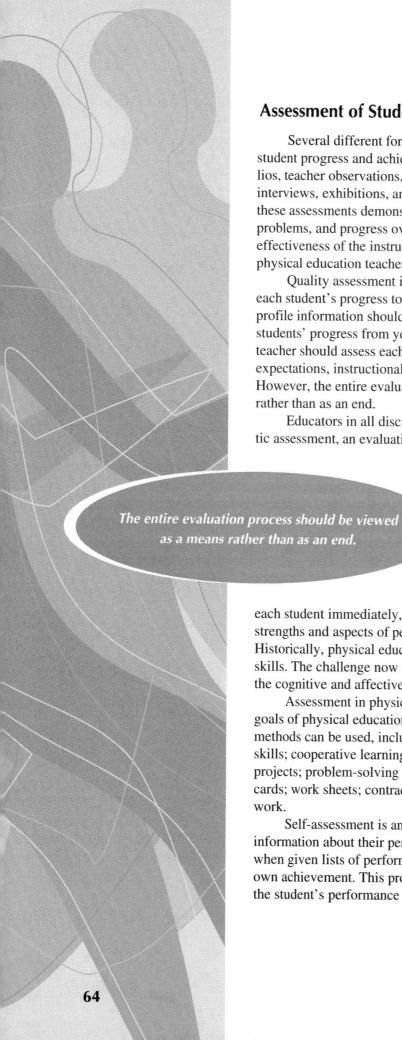

Assessment of Students

Several different forms of assessment can be used to measure student progress and achievement in physical education: student portfolios, teacher observations, performance tests, open-ended questions, interviews, exhibitions, and cooperative group projects. The results of these assessments demonstrate how children use skills, solve movement problems, and progress over time. Assessment can also reveal the effectiveness of the instructional program and provide insight into how physical education teachers can make learning more meaningful.

Quality assessment informs students, teachers, and parents about each student's progress toward the yearly learning expectations. Student profile information should be documented and maintained to monitor students' progress from year to year. At the beginning of each term, the teacher should assess each student to determine appropriate student expectations, instructional starting points, and grouping approaches. However, the entire evaluation process should be viewed as a means rather than as an end.

Educators in all disciplines are moving increasingly toward authentic assessment, an evaluation process that can contribute to a lively, active, and exciting learning experience for students. Authentic assessment engages students in challenges requiring the application of skills, knowledge, and attitudes. It requires students to explain or demonstrate how they can use what they have learned. The assessment, relevant feedback, and results are reported to each student immediately, together with a focus on the student's strengths and aspects of performance that may need improvement. Historically, physical education has always assessed fitness and motor skills. The challenge now is to find authentic assessment instruments for the cognitive and affective domains.

The entire evaluation process should be viewed as a means rather than as an end.

Assessment in physical education should address the three major goals of physical education presented in this framework. A variety of methods can be used, including written tests; videotaped performances of skills; cooperative learning activities; individual, small-group, and class projects; problem-solving tasks; small-group and class discussions; task cards; work sheets; contracts; small-group and class projects; and homework.

Self-assessment is another means of providing students with information about their performance. Students can apply self-evaluation when given lists of performance objectives and directed to judge their own achievement. This procedure can be facilitated by the videotaping of the student's performance for follow-up viewing by the student.

On a higher level self-assessment can offer opportunities for students to establish personal goals and make critical and valid evaluations as they monitor their progress. Establishing personal goals and practicing self-assessment should be an integral part of the students' learning experience in physical education. Self-assessment also helps motivate students to assume responsibility for their own learning.

Assessment in physical education should address the three major goals of physical education presented in this framework.

Peer assessment, which can be carried out by learners in pairs or groups, is an effective evaluation method for sixth grade or above. As students develop peer assessment skills, they learn the importance of giving and receiving support and constructive feedback. In peer assessment the student evaluator compares and contrasts another student's performance with the criteria established by the teacher. The results can be communicated orally or through the use of a task card, rating scale, or checklist. Peer assessment can be done live or can be videotaped.

Grades should bear a close relationship to the course goals and learning expectations. Course grades should not be used to report such elements as attendance, cleanliness, personality, punctuality, and wearing apparel. Assessment should require students to:

- Demonstrate an understanding of the application of information in new and familiar tasks.
- Explain *why* and *how* rather than merely perform movement.
- Integrate and connect understanding, analyze self-performances, observe others, and experiment with this knowledge.
- Demonstrate imagination, persistence, and creativity and show a capability for problem solving.

The physical education grade, based on the individual's progress toward the course objectives, should be included in the high school grade point average along with all other grades and should be accepted by colleges and universities.

Grading based on the achievement of clearly stated goals and objectives emphasizes what students know and can do. One form of grading involves an assessment instrument that describes a standard against which a piece of work or skill is judged. The assessment instrument tells the student what has to be accomplished. For the evaluation to be valid and fair, the student and evaluator must share a common understanding of what is to be accomplished. Throughout the semester students should be kept informed of their grades. Before any evaluation they should be provided with enough time for instruction and practice.

Performance Standards for Student Work

The following is a suggested example of generic performance standards for students' work at each of six possible performance levels that can be applied to any task or group of tasks. The three types of performances in physical education in which a student can achieve include purpose of task, understanding, and personal and social growth. In the statements in this chart, the overriding consideration, it must be emphasized, is achieving the purpose of the task rather than the elements of quality of performance in each level. (See also the section on students with disabilities in this chapter.)

Level	Standard to be achieved for performance at specified level
6	**Achieves purpose of the task fully while insightfully interpreting, extending beyond the task, or raising provocative questions** • Possesses motor skills, knowledge, and understanding requisite to success in physical activities and maintenance of a healthy life-style • Demonstrates skills, knowledge, and understanding • Models equitable and ethical behaviors toward others
5	**Accomplishes the purposes of the task** • Possesses the motor skills, knowledge, and understanding needed for success in physical activities • Selects activity appropriate to personal capabilities • Shows ability to accept and respect achievement level of self and others
4	**Completes purpose of the task substantially** • Displays movement proficiency with limited transfer of learning to other activities • Demonstrates willingness to experience new activities • Applies rules, vocabulary, strategy, and etiquette most of the time in activity
3	**Purpose of the task not fully achieved; needs elaboration; some strategies perhaps ineffectual or inappropriate; assumptions about the purposes perhaps flawed** • Movements more consistent but unreliable • Demonstrates limited acceptance of individual differences in self or others • Interacts positively most of the time with others in small groups

Level	Standard to be achieved for performance at specified level
2	**Important purposes of the task not achieved; redirection of work perhaps needed; completion affected by approach to task** • Movements inconsistent and unreliable • Ongoing affirmation required to attend to the task • Teacher direction required for basic cooperation
1	**Purposes of the task not accomplished** • Shows little evidence of ability to control or replicate a movement • Is unable to verbalize needs • Displays unstable, inappropriate, aggressive social behavior

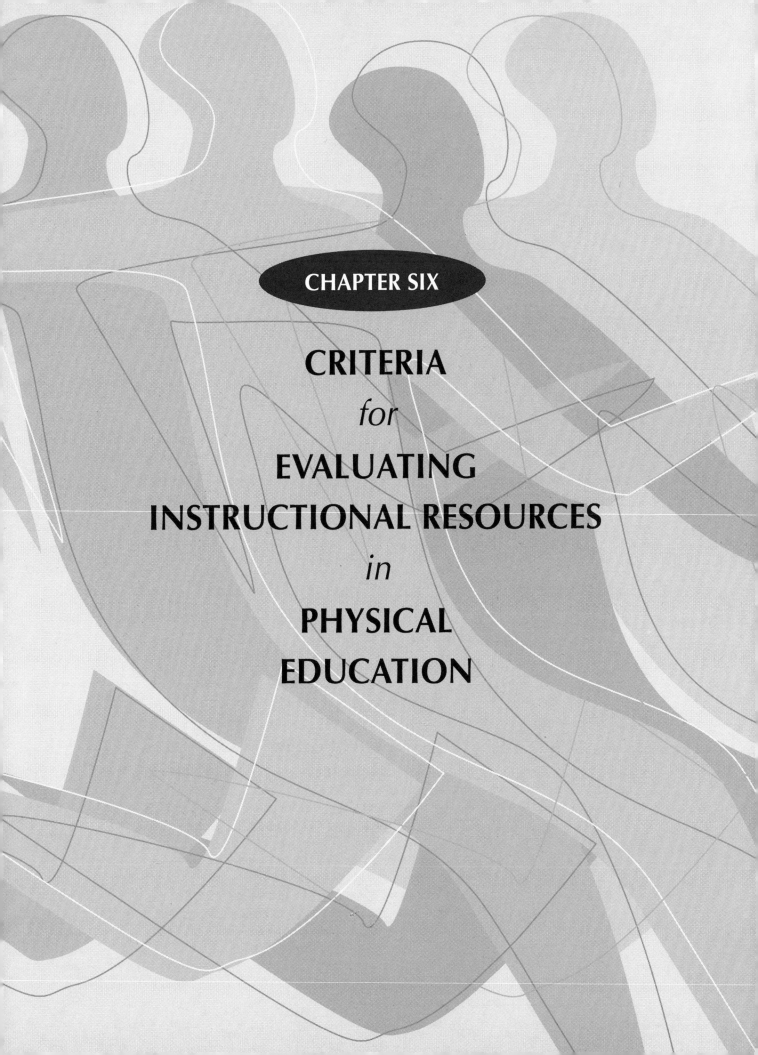

CHAPTER SIX

CRITERIA
for
EVALUATING
INSTRUCTIONAL RESOURCES
in
PHYSICAL
EDUCATION

CHAPTER SIX

The instructional resources criteria found in this chapter represent elements of a physical education program closely aligned with the goals and vision of this framework. The criteria are suggested for use in the review and evaluation of instructional resources in physical education. A basic program should include a description of the content of the resources as well as suggestions on how all students can be helped to gain access to that content and how the physical education teacher can be supported.

Content of Instructional Resources

Instructional resources should reflect and support the vision, goals, and grade-level guidelines described in this framework. All the goals should be addressed, with support from their respective disciplines. Resources should present physical education as a comprehensive, sequential system that promotes the physical, mental, emotional, and social well-being of each student. The presentation of resources should be open and engaging, and vocabulary should be incorporated to facilitate understanding for both teachers and students.

Students should be encouraged to acquire understanding and knowledge about the content and skills of physical education. They should be able to grasp the *why* as well as the *how* of what they are doing. They should also understand that the content areas (rhythm and dance, aquatics, combatives, outdoor education, team sports, individual and dual sports, tumbling and gymnastics, and fitness) are vehicles for developing and refining skills. The content and skill areas are the basis of physical education.

Instructional resources should reflect and support the vision, goals, and grade-level guidelines described in this framework.

The idea of competition should be introduced gradually in instructional resources as in the overall physical education program itself. Students should understand that competition equates with making the most of one's physical potential and capabilities in a positive, meaningful way.

Access to Instructional Resources

Instructional resources in physical education should recognize cultural diversity and reflect strategies that research and practice have shown to be successful in engaging all students in learning. For all students to participate fully, tasks and activities should be made accessible to all students through a variety of approaches.

Woven throughout, for example, should be a multicultural perspective promoting respect for the dignity and worth of all people regardless of their differences and building on the knowledge, attitudes, beliefs, and cultural and linguistic foundation that students bring to class. The instructional resources should include activities for all students, including students with disabilities.

Instructional guides should provide ways to make instruction for limited-English-proficient (LEP) students comprehensible, age-appropriate, and commensurate with their academic backgrounds. The provision of glossaries and summaries of key concepts in the students' primary language is one way of giving LEP students access to the physical education curriculum. The format of resources—including clear headings, subheadings, illustrations, photographs, graphs, and charts, all clearly labeled—can greatly increase the likelihood that all students will understand basic concepts. Such conventions are critical for students with special needs, such as LEP students.

The instructional resources should provide teachers with general and lesson-specific advice to support the learning of all students, including ways to:

- Connect the students' daily experiences with classroom activities.
- Encourage students to recognize and value the points of view and experiences of others where appropriate.
- Use peer support and cooperative learning groups.

- Use activities in which students experience both challenge and success.
- Make appropriate use of technology.
- Emphasize clearly that a desirable goal is for each individual to participate in a variety of pleasurable physical activities and to maintain an active life-style.

Support for the Teacher

Suggestions to aid the teacher should be based on current research on learning styles and effective instruction. Instructional resources should include, within the units of instruction, descriptions of the key goals and concepts of movement skills and movement knowledge; self-image and personal development; and social development. They should also include descriptions of what units should look like when implemented in the classroom and how experiences within units are related to what is known about the particular level of development being addressed.

Suggestions for working with diverse groups of students should also be included in instructional resources. Strategies should be offered for helping students work together productively and managing technology-based media and materials so that appropriate resources are available when students need to use them. Support for the teacher should also include ways to connect the student's daily environment and experiences with classroom activities.

Ways to connect physical education with other areas of the curriculum should be given careful consideration in instructional resources for physical education teachers. Support for the teacher in carrying out assessment should include models for assessing student performance, helping students assess their own physical performance, and using assessment results.

Because parental and community involvement is a part of a well-planned program, instructional resources should include suggestions for involving families and the community and keeping them informed about the program. Sample letters to family and community members about the value of the program, the rationale for what students are learning, and the instructional approaches being used might be included.

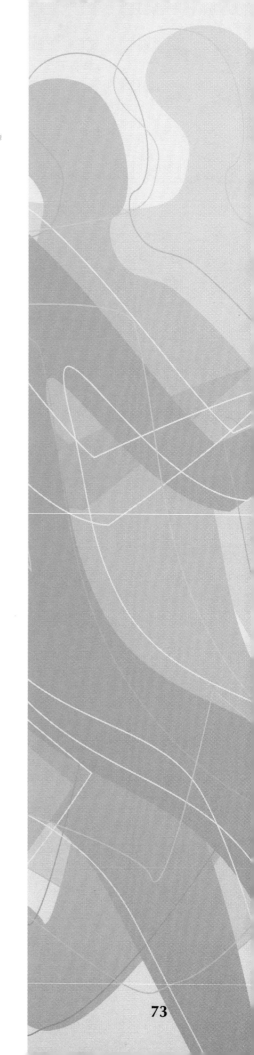

APPENDIX A

THE PHYSICALLY EDUCATED STUDENT: DEFINITION *and* OUTCOMES

The committee completed a definition of the physically educated student and identified the outcomes that clarify and amplify this definition. The attached document integrates the definitions and outcomes. For each of the five parts of the definition (HAS, IS, DOES, KNOWS, VALUES), there are attendant outcomes. The five parts of the definition represent the important learning related to the major learning domains (psychomotor, cognitive, and affective) found in physical education. The outcomes are inseparable from their parent definitional statements. Likewise, the five component definitional statements cannot be separated from each other. There is a kind of "all or none principle" involved in this product. The definition of the physically educated student depends upon the twenty outcomes, and the twenty outcomes have value only in relation to the definition's five components. The format in which the definition and outcomes are presented is the format in which they must be presented when reference is made to this effort.

If more students are to become "physically educated" in ways indicated by the definition and outcomes, then a daily, quality physical education program is required. One of the primary goals of this project has been to document the need for and importance of such programs.

Both the definition and the outcomes were approved by the NASPE's Association Delegate Assembly and the NASPE Cabinet. That the definition and outcomes already are making an impact on the profession is an indication of their value. For example, several states are using this document in their planning, and other organizations and agencies have taken action to endorse the definition and the outcomes. If the definition and outcomes help physical educators achieve greater consensus on and support for daily quality physical education programs, the NASPE goals for the project will be fulfilled.

Reprinted, with permission, from *Outcomes of Quality Physical Education Programs.* Reston, Va.: National Association for Sport and Physical Education, 1992, pp. 6–7.

Definition and Outcomes of the Physically Educated Person

Approved by NASPE Association Delegate Assembly—April, 1990

A Physically Educated Person

HAS learned skills necessary to perform a variety of physical activities

1. . . . moves using concepts of body awareness, space awareness, effort, and relationships.
2. . . . demonstrates competence in a variety of manipulative, locomotor, and nonlocomotor skills.
3. . . . demonstrates competence in combinations of manipulative, locomotor, and nonlocomotor skills performed individually and with others.
4. . . . demonstrates competence in many different forms of physical activity.
5. . . . demonstrates proficiency in a few forms of physical activity.
6. . . . has learned how to learn new skills.

IS physically fit

7. . . . assesses, achieves, and maintains physical fitness.
8. . . . designs safe personal fitness programs in accordance with principles of training and conditioning.

DOES participate regularly in physical activity

9. . . . participates in health-enhancing physical activity at least three times a week.
10. . . . selects and regularly participates in lifetime physical activities.

KNOWS the implications of and the benefits from involvement in physical activities

11. . . . identifies the benefits, costs, and obligations associated with regular participation in physical activity.
12. . . . recognizes the risk and safety factors associated with regular participation in physical activity.

13. . . . applies concepts and principles to the development of motor skills.

14. . . . understands that wellness involves more than being physically fit.

15. . . . knows the rules, strategies, and appropriate behaviors for selected physical activities.

16. . . . recognizes that participation in physical activity can lead to multicultural and international understanding.

17. . . . understands that physical activity provides the opportunity for enjoyment, self-expression, and communication.

VALUES physical activity and its contributions to a healthful life-style

18. . . . appreciates the relationships with others that result form participation in physical activity.

19. . . . respects the role that regular physical activity plays in the pursuit of lifelong health and well-being.

20. . . . cherishes the feelings that result from regular participation in physical activity.

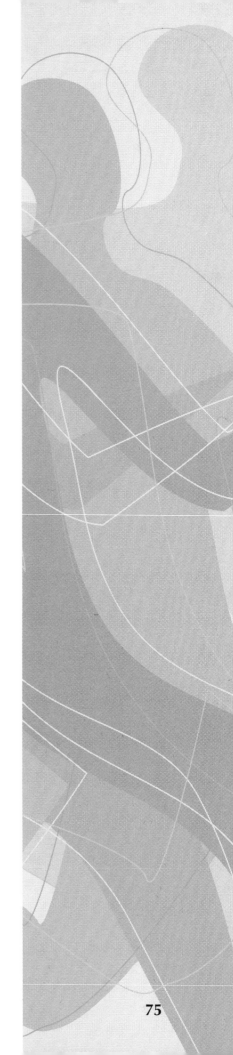

PROGRAM ADVISORY CLARIFYING ADAPTED PHYSICAL EDUCATION PROGRAM SERVICES

California Department of Education   SPD: 93/94-01   July 12, 1993

ATTENTION: County and District Superintendents of Schools
(Attention: Directors of Special Education)
County Coordinators and District Supervisors of Physical Education
Special Education Local Plan Area Administrators
Principals (High School, Middle School, and Elementary)

FROM: Shirley A. Thornton, Ed.D.
Deputy Superintendent
Specialized Programs

SUBJECT: **ADAPTED PHYSICAL EDUCATION PROGRAM SERVICES**

The California Department of Education recognizes that children with disabilities who are eligible for special education and related services have a right to a free and appropriate education to meet their unique needs. It is the purpose of this Program Advisory to describe the variety of physical education services available for children with disabilities. All children, unless excused or exempt under *Education Code* §51241, are required to have an appropriate physical education program. Availability of adapted physical education services, therefore, should be consistent in all districts, counties, and regions of the state. In addition, these services should be provided in such a manner that promotes maximum interaction between children with disabilities and their non-disabled peers. *EC §51210 and 51222.*

The California Department of Education recognizes that professional practices in physical education have been developed which are effective in providing quality services for children. The purpose of this advisory is to identify these practices, which could be used as guidelines. Various types of physical education programs and services are necessary to meet the needs of children and are to be made available as appropriate. For this instructional area, there is a need to:

• Address eligibility criteria.
• Outline a process for physical education programming.
• Ensure that appropriately qualified staff are employed, consistent with credentialing requirements.

- Address considerations unique to the demographics of various districts, counties, and special education local plan areas (SELPAs).
- Suggest guidelines for program eligibility, caseloads, and screening.

Questions and Answers

Types of Physical Education

Question: What are the various types of physical education programs available?
Answer:

General Physical Education

Full spectrum of game, sport, fitness, and movement activities. No adaptations or modifications required for safe and successful participation.

Modified Physical Education

Participation within general physical education by a physical education specialist or general classroom teacher but with modifications such as "no running," "no contact sports," "use of crutches," etc.
5CCR §3051.5(a).

Specially Designed Physical Education

Physical education programming for a special education class with minimal or limited adaptations provided for the children and taught by the person who normally teaches physical education for this population.
5CCR §3051.5(a).

Adapted Physical Education

Direct physical education services provided by an adapted physical education specialist to students who have needs indicated by an assessment and evaluation of motor skills performance and other areas of need. Children receiving adapted physical education, as indicated on the IEP, are included in the state and federal child count.
5CCR §3051.5(a).

Adapted Physical Education Collaboration

Physical education services in this option are provided and/or implemented jointly with other school staff members in order to assist children in meeting individualized goals, objectives, or needs through all options. Service delivery may be a transitional progression through the various stages or a combination of options offered simultaneously to meet individual needs. This may include some direct "hands-on" services, directly working with children, as part of the collaborative process. These children will be counted on the federal pupil count when direct services are provided on a regular basis by the adapted physical education specialist as indicated on the IEP.

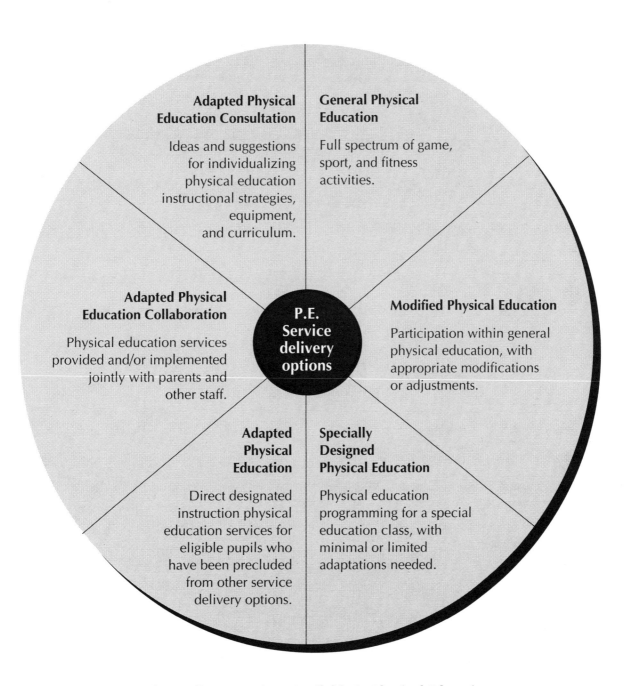

Adapted Physical Education Consultation

Ideas and suggestions for individualizing physical education instructional strategies, equipment, and curriculum.

General Physical Education

Full spectrum of game, sport, and fitness activities.

Adapted Physical Education Collaboration

Physical education services provided and/or implemented jointly with parents and other staff.

P.E. Service delivery options

Modified Physical Education

Participation within general physical education, with appropriate modifications or adjustments.

Adapted Physical Education

Direct designated instruction physical education services for eligible pupils who have been precluded from other service delivery options.

Specially Designed Physical Education

Physical education programming for a special education class, with minimal or limited adaptations needed.

Service Delivery Options Available in Physical Education

Adapted Physical Education Consultation

Assistance is given to parents, general and special class teachers, or general physical education teachers who are conducting either the general, modified, or specially designed physical education program. Ideas and suggestions for individualizing the instruction, resources, modifications or adaptations, and/or identifying supplementary devices/teaching aids that would facilitate the skills of an individual with exceptional needs may be shared. These services should be considered as support services provided by the adapted physical education specialist and do not include directly working with children and will not be recorded on the pupil count.

Identification Procedure

Question: How is the need for adapted physical education determined?

Answer:

A child must first be found eligible under 5CCR §3030(a-j), including the new federal categories of autism and traumatic brain injury. In addition, areas that may be addressed in the assessment plan to determine the need for physical education and the appropriate level of service include:

- impaired fine and/or gross motor skills.
- significant difficulty in motor functioning.
- cannot safely participate in general physical education.
- unable to accomplish motor skills attempted in any other type of instructional physical education programming tried, considered, or offered for this student in general, modified, or specially designed physical education.

In summary, a special education child who is identified with a disabling condition may receive adapted physical education if the need is documented in the assessment report(s) developed through EC §56320-56329 and the IEP team process. Temporary disabilities do not meet eligibility criteria.
EC §56026(e).

> "Temporary physical disability means a disability incurred while a pupil was a regular education child and which at the termination of the temporary physical disability, the pupil can, without special intervention, reasonably be expected to return to his or her regular education class."
> 5CCR §3001(v).

Criteria for Adapted Physical Education

Question: Are there statewide criteria for IEP teams to consider when determining the need for adapted physical education services?

Answer:

There are no specific state adapted physical education services criteria. However, once the child is identified as having a disabling condition which is affecting physical education performance and the child is determined to be eligible for special education by the IEP team, specific physical education services must be addressed as stated in 34 *Code of Federal Regulations* (CFR) §300.307.

Each special education local plan area (SELPA) is to develop policy and implementation procedures within their local plan which describe all Designated Instruction and Services (DIS), including adapted physical education. Additionally, each district, SELPA, or county office must ensure that a variety of physical education program options is available to meet the needs of children with disabilities for special education and related services. The California Department of Education, in conjunction with professionals in the field, recommends the following be considered when determining the appropriate physical education services(s) for eligible special education children.
EC §56200 and EC §56360.

Before a referral to special education is made, interventions, adaptations, and modifications within the existing general education program should be tried and documented. This includes general physical education when the area of motor skill ability is a factor in the possible disabling condition. Appropriate and meaningful intervention strategies should be based on the child's needs, age, and curriculum content and should be documented and reported for a designated period of time. These interventions should take place within the general physical education program for a child from a general education classroom.
EC §56303.

Referral

After reasonable modifications have been attempted and monitored, a determination may be made by the Student Study Team or similar site process that a child's needs might require adapted physical education services and the formal referral process is then initiated.

Assessment

Once referred, each individual child must have an assessment plan developed based on specific needs and areas of suspected disability. For physical education this could mean: gross motor skills, fine motor skills, perceptual motor skills, performance, and physical fitness. Assessment must address the individual child's needs and show specific attention to referral concerns. For example, what may be an appropriate measurement for a child with severe asthma in a regular class is not necessarily appropriate for a child with severe disabilities in a special day class who may require a more complex assessment battery. Formal assessment may not begin prior to receiving the written consent of the parent.
EC §56321.

Test Selection

There are a great number of variables in terms of the appropriateness of test selection, areas of need, functional skill issues, general motor skill differences, and integration/mainstream goals for each child. The assessment plan developed must address all areas related to the suspected disability on an individual basis.
EC §56320(f).

Assessments are used by adapted physical education specialists to establish a motor profile for referred children. These tests are used and reported in different units of measure. Assessment reports may include individual test data, documentation of modifications and interventions, review of records, reports, and class/child observations, present level of functioning, and recommendations. All this information may have a bearing on the selection of service delivery for the child.

If standardized tests are considered to be invalid for a specific child, the discrepancy shall be measured by alternative means as specified on the assessment plan. Best practice regarding assessment supports an ongoing process that begins with parents and teachers in the regular classroom and promotes assessments that are conducted using a variety of formal and informal measures within the home, school, and the community. It is critical that the assessments, procedures, and practices utilized are nonbiased and are attentive to the cultural and linguistic characteristics of each child.

Consideration for Adapted Physical Education

Question: When may a child be considered for adapted physical education services?

Answer:

The individual child may be considered for adapted physical education services if the IEP team determines that the child is eligible to receive special education and/or related services. After the IEP team determines the child is identified as an individual with disabilities pursuant to 5CCR §3030:

> "A child shall qualify as an individual with exceptional needs, pursuant to Section 56026 of the Education Code, if the results of the assessment as required by Section 56320 demonstrate that the degree of the child's impairment as described in Section 3030 (a through j) requires special education in one or more of the program options authorized by Section 56361 of the Education Code. The decision as to whether or not the assessment results demonstrate that the degree of the child's impairment requires special education shall be made by the individualized education program team, including assessment personnel in accordance with Section 56341(d) of the Education Code. The individualized education program team shall take into account all the relevant material which is available on the child. No single score or product of scores shall be used as the sole criterion for the decision of the individualized education program team as to the child's eligibility for special education. The specific policies and procedures for implementation of these criteria shall be developed by each special education local plan area and be included in the local plan pursuant to Section 56220(a) of the Education Code."
> *5CCR §303.*

The assessment may indicate a need for more intensive services or support. For some children, a physician's medical statement may become a part of the assessment information. There are no formalized eligibility criteria established in federal or state statute or regulation for adapted physical education. There are some test score variables that may indicate this need when a child scores:

- at least 1.5 standard deviations below the mean;
- below the 7th percentile for his or her chronological or developmental age on a norm-referenced or standardized test; or
- at or below 70 percent of his or her chronological age level in the motor skill areas.

Other Health Impaired

Question: What must be considered when a child is categorized as other health impaired (OHI)?

Answer:

Other health impaired (OHI) is one of the disabling conditions under which children may be determined eligible to receive special education. Current regulations state:

> "A child has limited strength, vitality or alertness, due to chronic or acute health problems, including, but not limited to, a heart condition, cancer, leukemia, rheumatic fever, chronic kidney disease, cystic fibrosis, severe asthma, epilepsy, lead poisoning, diabetes, tuberculosis and other communicable infectious diseases, and hematological disorders such as hemophilia which adversely affect a child's educational performance in accordance with Section 56026(e) of the Education Code, such physical disabilities shall not be temporary in nature as defined by Section 3001(v)."

A child's eligibility for special education and related services under OHI does not automatically ensure the child will receive adapted physical education. A child will receive adapted physical education if the results of the assessment demonstrate that the degree of the child's impairment requires special education and/or related services, developmental or corrective instruction and the child is "precluded from participation in the activities of the general physical education program, modified general physical education, or in a special class." A physician's statement that precludes physical activity/participation will exempt a child from participation in physical education.
5CCR §3051.5.

Unduplicated Adapted Physical Education

Question: May adapted physical education be the only special education service an individual receives?

Answer:

Yes. If the child qualifies as a child with disabilities, adapted physical education is a Designated Instruction and Service. It may then be provided to individuals or to small groups in a specialized area of instructional need, and throughout the full continuum of educational settings.
EC §56363, 5CCR §3051.

Role of the Adapted Physical Education Specialist

Question: What is the role of the adapted physical education specialist?

Answer:

The role of the adapted physical education specialist includes:

Assessing and Identifying a child's needs, recommending the appropriate physical education service delivery, and determining the present level of motor skill functioning. Once an IEP is developed, a child may be monitored by the adapted physical education specialist through all the options of physical education services, which could include adapted physical education, specially designed, modified, and general, until the child has mastered the skills necessary to participate independently in the general physical education program. The adapted physical education specialist may coordinate a combination of options offered simultaneously to meet the physical education requirements of the child.

Collaborating or Consulting with providers of general physical education, general physical education with modifications, or specially designed physical education programs. Children in a special education class may also receive direct service from an adapted physical education specialist if it is on the IEP.

Providing Direct Adapted Physical Education to children identified through the IEP team process who need adapted physical education services delivered in this manner. The initiation, frequency, and duration of the adaptive physical education services must be indicated on the IEP.

Local education agencies should ensure that "the person providing instruction and services shall have a credential authorizing the teaching of adapted physical education as established by the Commission on Teacher Credentialing."
5CCR §3051.5(b).

Role of Instructional Aides

Question: What is the role/use of instructional aides in adapted physical education?

Answer:

The role of the instructional aide in adapted physical education is to assist and supplement the adapted physical education specialist or assist the classroom teacher in carrying out supportive instruction in ". . . improving the quality of educational opportunity for children. . . ."
EC §45341.

The term "instructional aide" is defined in EC §45343.

". . . 'instructional aide' means a person employed to assist certificated personnel in the performance of their duties and in the supervision of pupils and in instructional tasks which, in the judgment of the certificated personnel to whom the instructional aide is assigned, may be performed by a person not licensed. . . ."

". . . these duties shall not include assignment of grades to pupils. An instructional aide need not perform such duties in the physical presence of the teacher, but the teacher shall retain his responsibility for the instruction and supervision of the child in his charge. . . ."
EC §45344.

Section 45347 emphasizes that instructional aides are to assist, not to replace certificated teachers:

"An instructional aide shall not be deemed a certificated employee for the purposes of apportioning state aid and no regrouping of pupils with instructional aides shall be construed as a class for apportionment purposes. . . ." (for example, DIS)
EC §45347.

The adapted physical education specialist is generally assigned responsibility for the supervision of the instructional aide in adapted physical education.

Consulation and Collaboration

Question: How should consultative and collaborative adapted physical education services be used?

Answer:

Consultative services are usually given to general and special education class teachers, general physical education teachers, and parents to help implement either the general, modified, or specially designed physical education program. Help is often given to facilitate individualized instruction or identification of supplementary devices/teaching aids that would further develop the skills of an individual with exceptional needs.

Consultative services provided by an adapted physical education specialist to another teacher or a regular classroom instructional aide does not fulfill or substitute for the direct adapted physical education instruction indicated on a child's IEP.

> ". . . Consultative services may be provided to pupils, parents, teachers, or other school personnel for the purpose of identifying supplementary aids and services or modifications necessary for successful participation in the regular physical education program or specially designed physical education programs."
> *5CCR §3051.5(a).*

Collaborative services may be provided for individuals with disabilities jointly with other staff members in order to assist the special education children in meeting their individualized goals, objectives, or needs whether in adapted, general, modified, specially designed physical education, or a combination of these service delivery options. Collaboration could be used to facilitate a progression through the various types of physical education services. It could also be used to coordinate combinations of physical education services provided simultaneously to meet the individual child's needs.

The intent of collaborative services is to assist the teacher in general or special education to individualize the instruction or identify supplementary devices that would facilitate development of the skills of an individual with disabilities; this assistance can also promote programming for the least restrictive environment. The initiation, frequency, and duration of the adapted physical education collaboration must be indicated on the IEP.

More Than One Type of Physical Education

Question: May a child who is receiving special education and/or related services participate in more than one of the types of physical education programs?

Answer:

Yes. An IEP team may assign an individual with disabilities to any combination of physical education services offered such as general, modified, specially designed, adapted, or consultation. Direct service adapted physical education may be provided for a portion of the required time to concentrate on the stated goals(s) and objectives. The remainder of the required number of minutes for physical education instruction may be provided in general, modified, and/or specially designed physical education for 200 minutes every 10 school days for elementary and 400 minutes every 10 days for secondary, with several opportunities for excused or exempt absence. An IEP team should determine if a child cannot meet the required minutes for physical education instruction and indicate this in the individualized education program.

EC §51222, 51241, 51246, 51210, and 34 CFR §300.307.

Providing a combination of service delivery options in both general and special education instruction encourages communication, cooperation, and collaboration among the professionals and fosters continuity in the child's instructional program. The general classroom teacher, general physical education teacher, or special day class teacher should be aware of the goal(s) stated on the IEP and should reinforce skills taught by the adapted physical education specialist. The IEP team should indicate on the IEP how coordination will occur between school personnel.

Caseload

Question: What should the adapted physical education caseload be?

Answer:

There is no maximum caseload established for adapted physical education in state or federal statute or regulation. Caseloads that prevent the adapted physical education specialist from providing the instruction in accordance with the time and frequency indicated on the child's IEP would be out of compliance with state and federal statute and regulation. Minimum caseloads or DIS of 20 for unduplicated or 39 for duplicated child count are utilized and identified in the Education Code for funding purposes only.

EC §56728.6.

Actual caseload numbers will vary based on a number of factors, including, but not limited to:

- Time needed for assessment and identification.
- The number of classes or contact hours needed to provide service to assigned children.
- Number of days per week each child receives services.
- The amount of time spent providing collaborative and consultative services for general physical education with modification and specially designed physical education.
- Case management. Unduplicated IEPs from general education where adapted physical education specialist are the case managers are far more time consuming.
- Travel time and distance between sites.
- Assignments: itinerant or on-site/home-based. The ability and time to maintain a work space, be flexible in scheduling, set up lessons, and provide planned lessons diminishes with multiple sites. For example, an itinerant teacher may have to physically move and do several setups a day, teach in different working environments, and utilize multiple teacher contacts at these sites in order to facilitate scheduling.

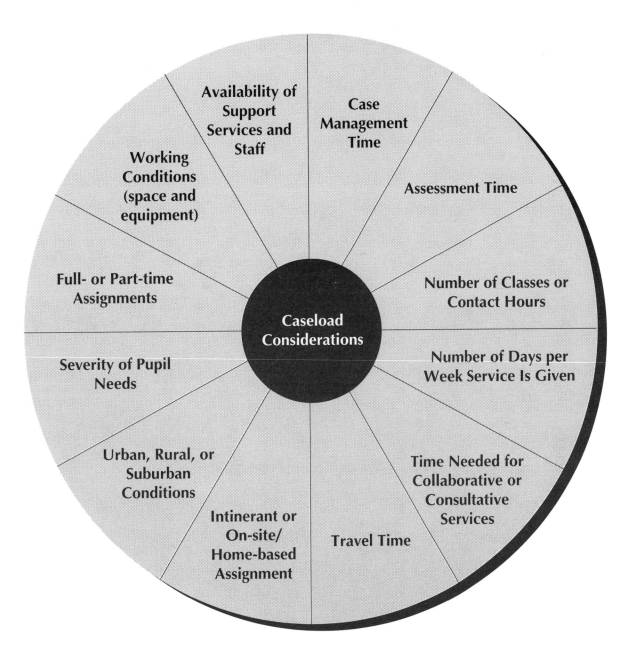

Factors to Consider in Establishing Caseload

- Urban, rural, or suburban conditions. The demographics of each of these conditions affect time needed for travel, parent contacts, and setting up teaching environments.
- Severity of disability of the children being served. Deaf-blind students are more challenging than students with a hearing loss.
- Assignments: full-time or part-time. Part-time teachers are often impacted with direct instruction time and need allocated time for non-instructional duties such as assessment, consultation, IEP meetings, screening, and report writing.
- Working conditions, including work space and equipment. Inadequate space and equipment requires additional time to make adjustments and adaptations in lessons and to utilize equipment.
- Availability of support services and support staff such as instructional aides, and clerical support.

Number of Sites

Question: What is the number of sites an adapted physical education specialist can effectively serve?

Answer:

There is no state or federally established number of sites that can effectively be served by an adapted physical education specialist. An appropriate number of sites would allow the adapted physical education specialist to provide effective instruction in accordance with the time and frequency indicated on the child's IEP and avoid noncompliance and due process issues.

Factors to consider when determining the number of sites an adapted physical education specialist can serve effectively are:

- Number of contact hours needed for each child, preschool through secondary.
- Severity of child needs.
- Travel time required.
- Number and size of groups or classes.
- Assessment time; different time allowances for duplicated versus unduplicated count.
- Time required for consultative and collaborative services.
- Case management and coordination among site administrators.

Screening and Assessment

Question: What types of screening are adapted physical education specialists permitted to do?

Answer:

Screening is available to all children; but because no state or federal statute or regulation defines the term "screening," many definitions exist. **Screening** should not be confused with **assessment**. Screening by the adapted physical education specialist may occur at any stage in the regular educational process. The screening process could include:

- Consultation with the classroom teacher or other school staff.
- School study team action plan.
- Home/parent activity program.

Screening may entail a review of any regular population such as a teacher's class or an entire grade level. In this traditional definition, regardless of the instrument used, children can respond in an individual setting as long as all within the common group receive the same treatment. The most common example of this type of screening is the mass testing of an entire classroom. All individuals in the class are seen for brief periods of time, often in the corner of the room or outside the classroom door. Since all members of a given population (for example; all kindergartners, second graders, or new children) receive the same treatment, this type of screening is not considered individual; nor is it targeted for a specific child. It is important for teachers to ensure that children are not singled out.

Assessment involves in-depth exploration of an individual's level of performance to identify disabilities and to determine eligibility for special education and related services. Individual assessment of a specific child must be conducted in accordance with federal and state statutes and regulations governing special education and related services, which include notification to the parent of the intent to assess, and obtaining written parental permission. *EC §56k001(j), 56320–22, 56324, 56327, and 56329.*

No Sole Criterion

Question: Can an adapted physical education specialist's evaluation be the sole criterion for entrance into a physical education program?

Answer:

No. Both federal and state statutes and regulations require that: assessment is made by a multi-disciplinary team, including at least one teacher or other specialist with knowledge in the area of the suspected disability, and that no single procedure can be used as the sole criterion for determining an appropriate educational program. The final programming and determination of the eligibility is made by the IEP team.
34 CFR 300.532(d), (e), EC 56320.

Occupational and Physical Therapy

Question: Is adapted physical education a substitute for occupational or physical therapy?

Answer:

No. Adapted physical education and occupational physical therapy serve different functions. A pupil may have both services. One is not a substitute for the other. For children under the age of three, adapted physical education may not be appropriate.

Infant, Toddler Adapted Physical Education

Question: Is adapted physical education appropriate for infants and toddlers under the age of three?

Answer:

For children under the age of three, individual developmental play activities should be infused into the daily or weekly curriculum or activities in the home or school. Adapted physical education support services may include collaboration and consultation to parents, staff, and other service providers. Assessment and/or recommendations for services for transition into a curriculum-based preschool program may be appropriate.

Summary Statement

This Program Advisory is designed to provide general guidelines and terminology common to all local education agencies, school sites, providers, and consumers. It is our intent to improve upon the consistency, content, and implementation concepts currently being utilized within the field of adapted physical education on a statewide basis. It is important to have correct and accurate information when designing and delivering all physical education service delivery options. Individual teachers and local education agencies may need assistance in identifying appropriate program options, expanding existing service delivery for more efficiency and effectiveness, and evaluating current program quality. For further information, contact:

	or	*or*

Janine Swanson
Consultant
California Department
   of Education
Special Education Division
P.O. Box 944272
Sacramento, CA 94244-2720
(916) 657-2692
	Kathryn Summa Aufsesser
	Special Education Department
	San Diego City Schools
	Dana Administrative Center,
	Rm. 232
	1775 Chatsworth
	San Diego, CA 92107-3209
	(619) 225-3772
		Dr. Perky Stromer
		Department of HPER
		California State Poly
		   University
		3801 W. Temple
		Pomona, CA 91768
		(909) 869-2776

This advisory represents the efforts of the late Jules Spizzirri, Special Education Consultant, Administrators of special education, and the Adapted Physical Education State Council of the California Association for Health, Physical Education, Recreation and Dance.

Publications Available from the Department of Education

This publication is one of over 600 that are available from the California Department of Education. Some of the more recent publications or those most widely used are the following:

Item No.	Title (Date of publication)	Price
1063	Adoption Recommendations of the Curriculum Development and Supplemental Materials Commission, 1992: California Basic Instructional Materials in Science (1992)	$5.50
0883	The Ages of Infancy: Caring for Young, Mobile, and Older Infants (videocassette and guide) (1990)*	65.00
0973	The American Indian: Yesterday, Today, and Tomorrow (1991)	6.50
1012	Attendance Accounting and Reporting in California Public Schools (1991)	5.50
1079	Beyond Retention: A Study of Retention Rates, Practices, and Successful Alternatives in California (1993)	4.25
0972	California Assessment Program: A Sampler of Mathematics Assessment (1991)	5.00
0912	California State Plan for Carl D. Perkins Vocational and Applied Technology Education Act Funds, 1991–1994 (1991)	13.00
1067	California Private School Directory, 1993-94 (1993)	16.00
1074	California Public School Directory (1993)	16.00
1017	California State Plan for the Child Care and Development Services Funded Under Federal Block Grant (1991)	5.50
1036	California Strategic Plan for Parental Involvement in Education (1992)	5.75
0488	Caught in the Middle: Educational Reform for Young Adolescents in California Public Schools (1987)	6.75
0874	The Changing History–Social Science Curriculum: A Booklet for Parents (1990)	10/5.00†
1053	The Changing History–Social Science Curriculum: A Booklet for Parents (Spanish) (1993)	10/5.00†
0867	The Changing Language Arts Curriculum: A Booklet for Parents (1990)	10/5.00†
0928	The Changing Language Arts Curriculum: A Booklet for Parents (Spanish Edition) (1991)	10/5.00†
0777	The Changing Mathematics Curriculum: A Booklet for Parents (1989)	10/5.00†
0891	The Changing Mathematics Curriculum: A Booklet for Parents (Spanish Edition) (1991)	10/5.00†
1072	Commodity Administrative Manual (1993)	13.00
0978	Course Models for the History–Social Science Framework, Grade Five—United States History and Geography: Making a New Nation (1991)	8.50
1034	Course Models for the History–Social Science Framework, Grade Six—World History and Geography: Ancient Civilizations (1993)	9.50
1045	Discoveries of Infancy: Cognitive Development and Learning (videocassette and guide) (1992)*	65.00
0976	Economic Education Mandate: Handbook for Survival (1991)	7.75
1046	English-as-a-Second-Language Model Standards for Adult Education Programs (1992)	7.00
0041	English–Language Arts Framework for California Public Schools (1987)	5.00
0927	English–Language Arts Model Curriculum Standards: Grades Nine Through Twelve (1991)	6.00
0987	ESEA, Chapter 2, Manual of Information (1991)	5.00
1056	Essential Connections: Ten Keys to Culturally Sensitive Care (videocassette and guide) (1993)*	65.00
1011	Exemplary Program Standards for Child Care Development Programs Serving Preschool and School-Age Children (1991)	5.50
0751	First Moves: Welcoming a Child to a New Caregiving Setting (videocassette and guide) (1988)*	65.00
0839	Flexible, Fearful, or Feisty: The Different Temperaments of Infants and Toddlers (videocassette and guide) (1990)*	65.00
0804	Foreign Language Framework for California Public Schools (1989)	6.50
0809	Getting in Tune: Creating Nurturing Relationships with Infants and Toddlers (videocassette and guide) (1990)*	65.00
1080	Guide and Criteria for Program Quality Review—Elementary (1993)	9.00
1078	Guide and Criteria for Program Quality Review—Middle Level (1993)	10.00
0986	Handbook for Teaching Korean-American Students (1991)‡	5.50
0734	Here They Come: Ready or Not—Report of the School Readiness Task Force (Full Report) (1988)	5.50
0712	History–Social Science Framework for California Public Schools (1988)	7.75
0750	Infant/Toddler Caregiving: An Annotated Guide to Media Training Materials (1989)	9.50
0878	Infant/Toddler Caregiving: A Guide to Creating Partnerships with Parents (1990)	10.00
0880	Infant/Toddler Caregiving: A Guide to Language Development and Communication (1990)	10.00
0877	Infant/Toddler Caregiving: A Guide to Routines (1990)	10.00
0879	Infant/Toddler Caregiving: A Guide to Setting Up Environments (1990)	10.00
0876	Infant/Toddler Caregiving: A Guide to Social–Emotional Growth and Socialization (1990)	10.00
1070	Instructional Materials Approved for Legal Compliance (1993)	10.50
1024	It's Elementary! Elementary Grades Task Force Report (1992)	6.50
0869	It's Not Just Routine: Feeding, Diapering, and Napping Infants and Toddlers (videocassette and guide) (1990)*	65.00
1107	Literature for History–Social Science, Kindergarten Through Grade Eight (1993)	8.00

*Videocassette also available in Chinese (Cantonese) and Spanish at the same price.

†The price for 100 booklets is $30; the price for 1,000 booklets is $230. A set of one of each of the parent booklets in English is $3; a set in Spanish is also $3.

‡Also available at the same price for students who speak Cantonese, Japanese, Pilipino, and Portuguese.

Item No.	Title (Date of publication)	Price
1066	Literature for Science and Mathematics (1993)	$9.50
1033	Mathematics Framework for California Public Schools, 1992 Edition (1992)	6.75
0929	Model Curriculum Standards, Grades Nine Through Twelve (1985)	5.50
0968	Moral and Civic Education and Teaching About Religion (1991 Revised Edition)	4.25
0969	Not Schools Alone: Guidelines for Schools and Communities to Prevent the Use of Tobacco, Alcohol, and Other Drugs Among Children and Youth (1991)	4.25
0974	Parent Involvement Programs in California Public Schools (1991)	6.75
0845	Physical Education Model Curriculum Standards, Grades Nine Through Twelve (1991)	5.50
1032	Program Guidelines for Individuals Who Are Severely Orthopedically Impaired (1992)	8.00
0906	Quality Criteria for High Schools: Planning, Implementing, Self-Study, and Program Quality Review (1990)	5.00
0979	Readings for the Christopher Columbus Quincentenary (1992)	2.75*
1048	Read to Me: Recommended Readings for Children Ages Two Through Seven (1992)	5.50
0831	Recommended Literature, Grades Nine Through Twelve (1990)	5.50
0895	Recommended Readings in Spanish Literature: Kindergarten Through Grade Eight (1991)	4.25
0753	Respectfully Yours: Magda Gerber's Approach to Professional Infant/Toddler Care (videocassette and guide) (1988)†	65.00
1042	School Nutrition Facility Planning Guide (1992)	8.00
1038	Science Facilities Design in California Public Schools (1992)	6.25
0870	Science Framework for California Public Schools (1990)	8.00
1040	Second to None: A Vision of the New California High School (1992)	5.75
0926	Seeing Fractions: A Unit for the Upper Elementary Grades (1991)	7.50
0970	Self-assessment Guide for School District Fiscal Policy Teams: Facilities Planning and Construction (1991)	4.50
0980	Simplified Buying Guide: Child and Adult Care Food Program (1992)	8.50
0752	Space to Grow: Creating a Child Care Environment for Infants and Toddlers (videocassette and guide) (1988)†	65.00
1014	Strategic Plan for Information Technology (1991)	4.50
1043	Success for Beginning Teachers: The California New Teacher Project, 1988–1992 (1992)	5.50
0920	Suggested Copyright Policy and Guidelines for California's School Districts (1991)	3.00‡
1044	Together in Care: Meeting the Intimacy Needs of Infants and Toddlers in Groups (videocassette and guide) (1992)†	65.00
0846	Toward a State of Esteem: The Final Report of the California Task Force to Promote Self-esteem and Personal and Social Responsibility (1990)	5.00
0758	Visions for Infant/Toddler Care: Guidelines for Professional Caregiving (1989)	6.50
0805	Visual and Performing Arts Framework for California Public Schools (1989)	7.25
1016	With History–Social Science for All: Access for Every Student (1992)	5.50
0989	Work Permit Handbook (1991)	7.75
1073	Writing Assessment Handbook: High School (1993)	9.25

*Also available in quantities of 10 for $7.50 (item number 9875); 30 for $20 (9876); and 100 for $60 (9877).
†Videocassette also available in Chinese (Cantonese) and Spanish at the same price.
‡Also available in quantities of 10 for $12.50 (item number 9940); 50 for $55 (9941); and 100 for $100 (9942).

Orders should be directed to:

California Department of Education
Bureau of Publications, Sales Unit
P.O. Box 271
Sacramento, CA 95812-0271

Please include the item number for each title ordered.

Mail orders must be accompanied by a check, a purchase order, or a credit card number, including expiration date (VISA or MasterCard only). Purchase orders without checks are accepted from governmental agencies only. Telephone orders will be accepted toll-free (1-800-995-4099) for credit card purchases only. Sales tax should be added to all orders from California purchasers. Stated prices, which include shipping charges to anywhere in the United States, are subject to change.

A complete list of publications available from the Department, including apprenticeship instructional materials, may be obtained by writing to the address listed above or by calling (916) 445-1260.

93-33 (003-0191-91) 84351–300 12-93 30M